PRAISE FOR
DOING GOOD GREAT

"In *Doing Good Great*, Doug Balfour provides numerous examples from around the globe that demonstrate how supporting and cultivating local innovation and growth is essential for poverty alleviation. I have personally witnessed and advocated for the powerful effect that investments in local communities can have within a region, and it is my great hope that this book is not only read, but that its ideas are applied, resulting in a global collaborative effort that produces sustainable change."

–**JOHN A. KUFUOR**, FORMER PRESIDENT, REPUBLIC OF GHANA

"Lots of 'experts' purport to know how to best use donors' funds to make a difference to the suffering of the world's most marginalized communities, but Doug Balfour is the real deal. He combines years of experience on the frontlines of humanitarian crises with an unmatched expertise in working with philanthropists to help them make a real impact with their funds. It's a powerful combination—and this compelling book shows how it can be done."

–**NICK GRONO**, CEO, THE FREEDOM FUND

"*Doing Good Great* is a highly engaging mix of riveting story and astute analysis, made all the more compelling because of the author's unique portfolio of experiences in the worlds of business, international development agencies, and private philanthropy. Doug Balfour writes honestly and passionately, and the result is a book I would heartily recommend to experienced development practitioners and philanthropic investors alike."

–**STEVE BRADBURY**, DIRECTOR, MICAH 6.8 CENTRE

"From the jungles of Liberia, via the boardrooms of England, and now back to transform some of the most challenging places on the planet, Doug Balfour defies the traditional orthodoxy of the philanthropy industry. His remarkable odyssey demonstrates that great results can flow from good intentions, especially when the creativity of an entrepreneurial spirit is disciplined by commercial rigor and led by a servant's heart. I've personally witnessed how the principles within this book can be applied in the real world, freeing more people to live joyful, healthy, and prosperous lives."

–**CHRISTOPHER L. CHANDLER**, FOUNDER AND CHAIRMAN,
 LEGATUM GROUP

"Doug Balfour is a transformational wizard. In *Doing Good Great*, he sets out the course for the long-term sustainability and relevance of philanthropy by making it an integral part of the constant innovation of the business models which are turning emerging markets into the economic powerhouses of the twenty-first century."

–**FERNANDO DE SOUSA**, GENERAL MANAGER, MICROSOFT 4AFRIKA

"Doug Balfour's book not only encourages and inspires readers to move from doing good to doing great, it does something far more important—it illustrates how."

–**KATHERINA M. ROSQUETA**, FOUNDING EXECUTIVE DIRECTOR,
 CENTER FOR HIGH IMPACT PHILANTHROPY & ADJUNCT FACULTY,
 SCHOOL OF SOCIAL POLICY & PRACTICE, UNIVERSITY OF PENNSYLVANIA

"Doug is a pioneer in creating development programs that connect donors and beneficiaries in meaningful and groundbreaking ways. This book shows how the fields of philanthropy and international development can work together to combat poverty and address many other challenges facing the world."

–**KARI STOEVER**, GLOBAL HEALTH AND DEVELOPMENT EXPERT

"Working out how to do philanthropy in a way that makes a genuine difference is one of the biggest challenges facing the world. Part memoir, part a how-to guide, Balfour has written an engaging, insightful, and practical book on what it takes to be a performance philanthropist."

–**MATTHEW BISHOP**, GLOBALISATION EDITOR, *THE ECONOMIST* &
COAUTHOR, *PHILANTHROCAPITALISM*

"In *Doing Good Great*, Doug Balfour draws on his decades of experience in philanthropy and business to do the great service of presenting us with a compelling work that will have you asking questions about how we as a society can hold ourselves to a higher standard of generosity. This is a worthy struggle and I am grateful for Doug's invitation to a deeper exploration of how best to care for those who are in deepest need."

–**GARY A. HAUGEN**, PRESIDENT & CEO, INTERNATIONAL JUSTICE MISSION

"As a newcomer to the world of charitable giving, I was looking for 'the book' on how to give effectively to get the most return for each dollar donated. In *Doing Good Great*, Doug writes a practical guide for donors and distills several decades of knowledge accumulated from underwriting, structuring, and measuring thousands of charitable grants to organizations."

–**KEITH COCKRUM**, PRIVATE DONOR

"This book doesn't just offer a theory of change, but provides proven solutions to some of the world's most neglected concerns."

–**ELLEN AGLER**, CEO, THE END FUND

"Balfour tells us how to give better, not just more. Journey with him as he shares eight pillars of how to maximize giving for excellent philanthropic outcomes. Experience how he deploys capital to create good."

–**JOANN FLETT**, DIRECTOR, MBA ECONOMIC DEVELOPMENT PROGRAM, EASTERN UNIVERSITY

"Doug Balfour's *Doing Good Great* illustrates the benefits of applying business's best practices to philanthropy and engaged collaboration. Balfour tells his exciting narrative, demonstrating how to make a truly impactful difference in the face of dangerous adversity. His stories of love and commitment to effective philanthropy is a guide light for doing good great."

–**TIM MCCARTHY**, CMO, THE BUSINESS OF GOOD

"*Doing Good Great* not only shares the joys, challenges, and triumphs of one man's journey to change the world, but provides a practical guidebook for how we can all make a significant impact on the world in which we live."

–**BEN KEESEY**, CEO, INVISIBLE CHILDREN

DOING GOOD GREAT

An Insider's Guide to Getting the Most
out of Your Philanthropic Journey

DOUG BALFOUR

Published by Geneva Global
115 Bloomingdale Avenue, Wayne, PA 19087
ISBN: 978-0-9863771-0-5
Library of Congress Control Number: 2015930132

Design and illustration by Pixel Parlor.

Inasmuch as this book represents what I have learned over the last thirty years and who I have become, it is no overstatement to say that I owe all the good bits, the worthwhile parts, and most of the fun stuff in sharing this journey of discovery with my soul mate, wife, and partner, Anna, without whom I doubt I would have been as sane, as whole, and as balanced as I am. And for everyone who knows me, is that not a frightening prospect?

CONTENTS

PART ONE

GOOD IS NOT GOOD ENOUGH

I WISH MORE PEOPLE OF MEANS were not satisfied with just doing good in the world.

Don't get me wrong; I'm not discouraging anyone from using his or her money to help make a difference. But the needs out there are simply too vast to settle for making only a moderate impact.

Millions live without clean water, access to basic health care, or enough food. Millions die from diseases that are treatable and preventable. Infant-mortality rates remain unacceptably high in many places, while incomes are unconscionably low. Men, women, and children are bought and sold like disposable goods.

None of us in the West can hide from the terrible realities in other parts of the world. The latest tragedies and needs bombard our televisions, computers, and even cell phones daily.

The good news is that research suggests that the number of people living in extreme poverty—which means surviving on less than $1.25 a day—has gone down over the past twenty years or so by over 25 percent.[1] The bad news is that there are still more than one billion people living in impoverished conditions.

Those with means are responding generously to the needs. But neither goodwill nor the good intention of spending large amounts of money on problems and hoping they will go away is enough to bring about the level of change we must see.

---

1. "Rethinking Poverty: Report on the World Social Situation 2010," United Nations, accessed December 2, 2014, http://www.un.org/esa/socdev/rwss/docs/2010/chapter2.pdf.

Doing Good Great

Just as the answer to improving your business is to work smarter rather than simply harder, giving better, not just giving more, is the answer to making the world a better place. We need to do great, not just do good.

Geneva Global, the company I own, was founded to make that a reality, to bring a more disciplined and businesslike approach to charitable efforts, and to develop an investment mind-set in the world of need. We want to help people give in a way that makes their money work as hard as possible. We call it performance philanthropy—doing good better. Doing great.

The unique approach we have developed over the years has been sought out by foundations, wealthy individuals, financial advisers, nonprofits, and government and nongovernmental agencies. Our work with and for them has impacted hundreds of millions of beneficiaries over the past fifteen years or so.

We have helped clients make a significant difference in a wide range of concerns, from disaster relief and orphan care to providing clean water and rescuing child prostitutes. Through our direct management of over $140 million in grants to more than 1,700 projects on behalf of donors, as well as our work with clients to build and manage philanthropic partnerships resulting in nearly $1.4 billion for development programs, we have identified eight pillars to maximizing impact—principles that are crucial to consider when making a sizable investment in the betterment of the world.

Due diligence, detailed planning, careful monitoring, collaborative action, and creative thinking are just some of the foundations upon which we have built Geneva Global's unique approach. These principles come, in part, from lessons I have learned in my quarter-century of international development work and leadership. But the principles we have identified at Geneva Global have also been forged by the ideas and experiences of many others with whom I have worked and partnered, from successful business leaders to selfless field workers.

Though Geneva Global's innovative leadership in the area of international philanthropy has been the subject of articles by leading think tanks, banks, and financial media, we do not pretend for one moment we have enjoyed the success we have seen solely because of our efforts. Any credit we have been given should be shared with others also concerned with making more of a difference. That is entirely appropriate because, when it comes to dealing with the issues that face us on planet Earth, no single person, organization, or government is going to be wise or wealthy enough to do it all alone.

In fact, collective responsibility and collective action is at the heart of our approach. It will take all of us, working together, to make the world a better place for everyone.

I'm grateful that you are interested in being a part of the answer to some of our pressing global problems. So together, let's take up the challenge and determine to find ways to do good great. I hope that the following pages may help you discover how you can do that.

COUNTING THE COST

WHEN THEY CAME FOR ME AROUND MIDNIGHT, I thought that I was going to die.

After all, nobody went out after dark in Liberia. The worst of the brutal civil war may have been over, but the country was still chaotically unstable, with a strong undercurrent of violence. Once the sun set, ordinary citizens hunkered down in their homes, waiting for the relative safety of another dawn.

Even the heavily armed military avoided moving about once night fell if they possibly could. Driving up in the dark to a remote checkpoint like the one I had been arrested at earlier was just too dangerous. Poorly trained, ill-disciplined, and commonly high on drugs of some kind, the teens passing for soldiers were all too likely to shoot first and not even think to ask questions later.

So when they came into the shabby room where I'd been left for hours with Edward, my companion, and ordered us at gunpoint to follow them outside, I figured that we were going to be taken into the bush somewhere and killed.

They'd have to hide our bodies and get rid of our vehicle so there would be no evidence that a couple of nongovernmental organization (NGO) workers had arrived at the checkpoint they were manning. Then they would be able to keep the seven thousand Liberian dollars they had confiscated while accusing us of working for America's CIA and committing "economic espionage"—whatever that was.

I'd always managed to navigate these tricky waters on my many previous trips to the country's interior. The road from the Liberian capital, Monrovia, to southeastern Sinoe County was actually in pretty good condition when measured against the rest of the country's infrastructure, a good two-lane ribbon of asphalt, but it would take all day to make the 411-mile trip.

The delays came at the sixteen checkpoints dotted along the way. Manning them were members of Charles Taylor's so-called army, most of them kids fourteen to eighteen years of age. Just a year or so earlier, they had been the rebels, but when their leader was swept up into power, the tables were turned.

It had been a bloody, barbaric change of guard for the West African nation. Politics and ethnic rivalries exploded in an orgy of bloodletting when rebels overthrew longtime president Charles Doe, who had taken control by force years earlier. Even before Doe was toppled, those looking to unseat him were themselves divided, with Taylor and his one-time senior commander, Prince Johnson, leading opposing forces. With so many factions, the country remained tense even after the Economic Community of West African States Monitoring Group (ECOMOG), a multilateral West African peacekeeping force, took control of Monrovia.

Such was the situation when I arrived in April 1991 with my wife, Anna, and our two small children. We were leading a multinational team of a dozen volunteers with Medair, a Swiss-based organization, in the hope of bringing some help and relief in the form of war-trauma counseling and essential drugs to a wounded people.

The stories were horrifying and horrifyingly common. We heard of soldiers betting on whether a pregnant woman was carrying a girl or a boy and then slicing her open to pull the child from her womb to find out. Parents decapitated in front of their children. Parents forced to watch as their children were hacked to pieces before their eyes. Children forced to murder their parents.

Much of the carnage had been wreaked by children themselves—press-ganged into service, deliberately and brutally desensitized, and then fueled by cocaine and other drugs. Now with some of the rebel forces disbanded, some of these young killers were being held in detention at the capital's soccer stadium.

One of our roles was to try to find some way of helping these kids process all they had done and experienced, and to train others to do so as well. Among those in the country's limited government services, there was little or no awareness of the massive psychological wounds that the children were dealing with or how to treat them. Back home in England, Anna had been a clinical psychologist, so she met with Liberian government, church, and other community leaders to assess the situation and develop a program to help tackle some of the counseling needs.

Signs of the conflict that claimed an estimated quarter of a million lives were seen all around Monrovia. While walking along the beach one morning during an assessment visit several months before leading our team in, I'd kicked something with my foot. Looking down into the sand, I saw that I'd upturned a human skull. Later we heard that many were killed by firing squads on the beach.

But despite all this, Monrovia itself was now relatively safe and calm under the guard of troops from ECOMOG. With the help of a wide range of NGOs, health services were also being slowly reestablished across the country.

Things were not as good in parts of the interior where security was less certain, the infrastructure weaker, and Taylor still ruled. That is what had been taking me down to Sinoe County to deliver the monthly funds needed to support the work of our team members there. They were helping get abandoned health clinics up and running again to serve a population of around fifty thousand scattered across almost four thousand square miles.

These clinics provided simple medicines like aspirin and chloroquine. It wasn't sophisticated or elaborate health care, but for people in a malaria-ridden area that had not seen any medicine in more than two years, it was a lifesaving program.

NAVIGATING THE CHECKPOINTS was always challenging. The degree to which I had to blend diplomacy and determination would vary, according to how bored or stoned the young guards were and whether they were feeling the need to impress others with how much authority they had. Given that they would be brandishing AK-47s and other guns all the while, these encounters could be tense.

The roadblocks were thrown up at intervals, usually close to one of the small towns or villages along the road. The soldiers would commandeer an abandoned gas station, a community building, or a large house and set up their control center. Then they would bundle poles and other debris on the road to force vehicles to stop.

We'd slow down, giving those ahead a chance—we hoped— to see the big red "Medair NGO" signs displayed on our Toyota Hilux to signal that we were aid workers. Sometimes that would be enough for us to get waved through perfunctorily. Other times, not, in which case they'd ask to see our documentation and then want to know what we were doing.

I'd explain that we were helping their fellow Liberians by providing much-needed health care. Then the conversation would come round to the question of taxes—in other words, the bribes that were required of anyone who wanted to pass. The locals paid because they knew they had no choice, but we had a strict policy of not greasing anyone's palms.

At this point, it was always a bit of a delicate dance. I'd try to be firm but funny at the same time; a little spontaneous humor usually helped lubricate the hinges. It was important to keep the atmosphere light while at the same time showing just the right amount of respect. Sometimes the checkpoint guards would laugh, or they might half jokingly accuse me of being with the CIA. On other occasions, they'd tell me that they knew the only reason we were in the country was because we were getting paid very well.

I was tempted to tell them that, no, actually, no one in Medair got paid a salary and that, as volunteers, we had actually raised most of our own funds to be there. But I knew that it was best just to stick to my script: no, we were not in league with anyone; we were an independent NGO there to simply help the people of Liberia.

I'd actually been arrested several times on earlier trips. This usually consisted of being taken by an armed escort to meet with one of the group's so-called generals and then being grilled a little more before finally being allowed on my way. It was all a bit of a game, albeit with a dangerous and menacing edge.

The rules changed on me this time, however, when it came to the part about the money.

With a somewhat functioning government in Monrovia but the rest of the country in the hands of opposing forces, Liberia actually had two currencies in use. The "old" money was accepted in the interior of the country, but it was forbidden in the capital. Possession of "new" money in the interior was seen as evidence that you were a spy. We always made sure to count through the wad of money we were carrying before we set off from Monrovia, weeding out any incriminating new bills.

Maybe we were careless this time. Most likely some of the soldiers determined that this was the day they'd get rich and decided to stack the deck. As they looked through the wad of bills I had handed over after pulling it from the waist pouch hidden under my shirt, one of them began waving a "new" five-dollar bill and shouting.

I wasn't too worried at first when Edward, my Liberian team member, and I were arrested and shuffled off to the local command post in Salala. They took me into a dark back room and sat me down on a hard chair. Several soldiers stood around, waving their guns, as the leader began to accuse me of economic espionage.

I tried to remain calm and simply repeat the facts of who I was and why I was there. But as the questions continued and the afternoon dragged on beyond the time when they'd always previously gotten bored with the game and let me go, I became concerned.

9

Eventually I was taken to another room and left there with Edward. We were tired and hungry. Through the wall, we could hear the raised voices of the young men who had stopped us. Neither of us understood the tribal tongue, but there seemed to be an increasingly heated debate going on. I began to suspect that they were arguing about what to do with the money and how to get rid of us.

I attempted to reassure Edward, telling him that everything would work out. We tried to raise our spirits by singing some church songs we both knew, like the apostle Paul and his companion Silas did in the New Testament when they were thrown into jail. When we ran out of songs, we were left with our thoughts.

Mine turned to Anna and the children back in Monrovia. I wondered when she would learn that we hadn't made it to Sinoe County and how she would cope. I thought about my daughter, Alex, whose fourth birthday was coming up in twelve days' time, and my youngest child, Jonathan, just twenty-one months old.

Family and some friends had been worried when Anna and I told them we were taking our young family into the immediate aftermath of a war zone. We'd considered the risks but felt that we had something to offer, some way of helping, that made it worthwhile. Now I asked myself, had I done the right thing? Would I ever see my family again?

IT SEEMED THE ANSWER WAS NO when the door was pushed open and the soldiers came in with guns to take us out into the night. They didn't say where we were going or what was happening. If I hadn't been so anxious, I might have been tempted to laugh when they then told me I had to drive because they didn't have a vehicle.

With several of them jammed into our Toyota and holding guns to my head, I drove off, directed to the next village. Once there, I parked while some of them got out and disappeared into a hut—stashing the confiscated money somewhere, I figured. Then I was ordered to drive on.

I had no idea where we were going, but we drove for more than an hour, stopping at other checkpoints. At one, those on duty began firing their guns in the air. Maybe they would kill me before my abductors got to, I thought. The two groups began shouting at each other, brandishing their weapons. And then, thankfully, the skirmish ended, and we drove on.

Eventually we arrived at what I later learned to be the Liberian National Security Agency (NSA) headquarters run by Taylor's cousin. Pulled from the Toyota, I was manhandled and marched to a cell and then thrown in with the door locked behind me. I didn't know what had happened to Edward, who had been taken elsewhere.

As my eyes adjusted, I could make out some of my surroundings. The windows were cracked, the mosquito screens were full of holes, and hungry mosquitoes circled my head. It was dark, but I could just see a figure lying on the sole, very thin mattress in the cell. Awakened by my entrance, the man turned to look at me. I tried all the pidgin languages I knew, but he just looked blankly at me before turning over and going back to sleep.

There comes a point when you are so exhausted that you just can't physically continue feeling scared, so I lay down and went to sleep too.

The next morning I found myself aching, thirsty, hungry, and alone—no sign of my cell mate. Someone brought me some water, but otherwise I was left alone through the morning, my concern rising again. Finally, around midday, more than twenty-four hours since I was first arrested, I was told it was time to meet the commander.

Knowing Taylor's reputation for brutality, a meeting with one of his family and trusted deputies did not fill me with confidence. I was surprised to be led into a well-appointed office where the commander sat behind a desk. Nearby stood another man whose presence was unexpected. He was white.

"Why are you here?" the commander asked me. "What's going on?"

I wanted to ask him the same question, but I was too tired and uncertain to be sarcastic. I told the commander all that had happened. Then fear gave way to farce.

The white man turned out to be a representative of the United Nations, which oversaw NGO relations in the country, and he pressed for my release. The head of the NSA apologized after hearing my story. The soldiers should never have tried to take money from a relief agency, he said, and they would be taught a lesson. They would be arrested and dealt with, but would I mind driving his security detail there, as they had no working vehicles available right now?

So began a Keystone Kops–like retracing of my previous night's terrifying journey. We stopped at the village where I presumed the money had been hidden. Several of those who had detained me were rounded up and beaten. Some soldiers searched one of the huts and came out with about two-thirds of the money, which was eventually handed back to us. Then I was asked to drive the newly detained culprits back to the NSA headquarters.

On the way, we pulled over so some of those on board could relieve themselves by the side of the road. The ringleader of the checkpoint group seized his chance and made a break for the jungle. The other soldiers opened fire on him as he ran, but he escaped into the thick undergrowth unscathed as bullets whizzed around him.

Having dropped off the remaining group, Edward and I were finally sent on our way—this time with an NSA escort. With his presence, we blew through the rest of the roadblocks to get to our original destination in Sinoe County in record time.

IN THE TWENTY-FIVE YEARS since that nerve-racking incident, I have traveled to more than sixty other countries. I've witnessed some of the worst of what people can do to others and the best of what people can do for others.

I have been in some other risky situations: riding an overland bus through the Khyber Pass out of Afghanistan, ahead of advancing Taliban forces and standing by with families in a remote South Sudanese village, ready to evacuate at a moment's notice, as a slash-and-burn rebel group headed our way.

I have also mourned those who have died while working to help others. During our time in Liberia, Anna and I befriended Sean Devereux, a fellow Brit who was working through another agency to help children affected by the war. He was imprisoned one time as well and eventually forced to leave the country sometime after we did because of escalating violence.

Sean went to work for UNICEF, the United Nations Children's Fund, in Somalia, where just a few months after arriving, he was killed by a gunman hired by one of the many warlords in the northern port city of Kismayo.

Later, as head of one of Britain's largest relief charities, I and my staff grieved the deaths of four coworkers lost to accidents, a terrorist hijacking, and sickness out in the field.

Such losses weigh heavily, of course. For anyone's life to be cut short is a terrible thing. But even as I look back on my own brush with death and other moments of fear, the question that comes to mind is not, *Is it worth it?*

It's, *How worth it can we make it?*

From fighting malaria in an isolated corner of Liberia to now playing a part in eliminating a cabal of tropical diseases across large parts of Africa, I've come to believe that we all have a responsibility to help those who, for different reasons, are less able to help themselves.

Truly acknowledging their rights and the risks taken by those who serve them demands that our investments—of money, people, and resources alike—produce the best returns possible. That is what we call performance philanthropy.

And that is why it matters.

FANNING THE FLAMES

I HAVE SPENT MOST OF MY WORKING LIFE trying to help people in one way or another. But I didn't set out to change the world. In fact, the first time I left the comfort of the West, I wasn't looking to make a difference; I was hoping to make a fortune.

A newly recruited diamond hunter, I arrived in South-West Africa, what is now Namibia, as a lanky twenty-one-year-old with a degree in geology and some personal baggage. I was given a pump-action shotgun, a one-week crash course in management, and a sobering introduction to the ugly realities of injustice, inequality, and institutional neglect.

Within six months of my arrival, I found myself essentially running a remote part of the country. After some rudimentary orientation, I had been left in charge of an exploration project for De Beers, the world's biggest diamond company. That meant overseeing the entire operation near Tsumkwe, a settlement in the Kalahari Desert in the northeastern Otjozondjupa region. It was a dusty twelve- or thirteen-hour 4x4 ride from the capital, Windhoek.

We were running two searches: one near our main site and another a ninety-minute drive farther into the deserted bush near a place called Sigeriti. Between the two sites, there were around ninety workers, plus thirty families of some of the senior staff. Located in a large conservation area, it wasn't unusual to have leopards and lions wander through the camp at night. That was one reason for the weapon I'd been handed.

Though I'd been trained to study rocks, I found I was also expected to handle supplies, rations, and payroll. And being three hours' drive from the nearest town and any law-enforcement officials and radio the only communication link to them, I was also the de facto authority. (Another reason for the shotgun.)

I'd discovered geology as a teenager and had loved how it tied together my different interests. I enjoyed being out in the open, and I had a fascination for figuring out what lay below the surface. I didn't just look at rocks as two-dimensional surface outcrops but could envisage them as parts of often-hidden three-dimensional forms yet to be understood and marveled at.

Geology gave me a new way of looking at the world. I learned how rocks shape geography, which in turn determines where people live and what they do. Being a geologist is a bit like being a detective, I found. The rocks you can see are sort of tips of an iceberg; you don't really know what's underneath. So you take what you do know and try to apply it to what could be, matching what is and what might be—the facts and the possibilities—looking for the best answer.

When I obtained my degree from Southampton University, I certainly didn't see how it might be applied to something like international development. All I knew was that I didn't want to use my degree to look for oil; sitting on a rig out at sea for weeks at a time sounded really boring. Seismology demanded a stronger science bent than I had, so that left the hard rocks— looking for metals, precious stones, and diamonds.

An avid reader while at school, I'd enjoyed Wilbur Smith's *Gold Mine*, a thriller set in South Africa, and Hammond Innes's *Campbell's Kingdom*, an action novel set in the Canadian wilderness. Both featured geologists who, it seemed to me, had great adventures, made it rich, and got the girl. So sign me up.

Unfortunately girls turned out to be in short supply in my corner of South-West Africa. And the rugged realities of life there were not quite so Indiana Jones–like. Racial tensions were strong a decade before the country would win independence from neighboring South African rule. While political apartheid did not exist where I was as explicitly as it did across the border—where Nelson Mandela was still in a cell on Robben Island—it made its mark. The whites had the money, and that put them in charge.

Though most of our black workers were diligent and industrious, there was an undercurrent of anger and resentment. The country was in the midst of an armed struggle for independence, and our exploration sites were along one of the main routes taken by freedom fighters snaking their way down from Angola to launch attacks on white farmers. It was unspoken, but we knew where our laborers' ultimate sympathies lay.

I was also uncomfortable with some of the things I heard my small group of white colleagues say about the black employees. I'd grown up in a fairly mixed cultural neighborhood in England, and the open prejudice I found in South-West Africa shocked me. But initially I was too busy trying to keep on top of everything I had to learn and do to pay much attention.

I SOON REALIZED that being in charge meant acting confident, even if I wasn't. One time a bunch of my African workers drove into Tsumkwe on an errand, and when they came back, they were all blind drunk. So I fired sixteen of them on the spot.

Then I learned that one of our mechanics was a bit too quick with his hands. He wasn't just keeping things running, he was dipping into the cash box. When summoned and confronted, he stared at me across the workshop. I told him what I'd learned and that I was letting him go right away. He looked at me menacingly and fingered a large knife he had on him.

Inside I was terrified, but I ignored the threatening gesture and kept talking. I told him he had to leave immediately and not to bother asking me for a reference.

He glared at me. "I'm going across the border," he said. "I'm going to get an AK-47, and I am going to come back and kill you in your sleep."

I tried to remain calm. "Well, that's up to you," I replied. "But you still need to be on the truck that's leaving now."

For the next couple of weeks, I'd double-check that the loaded shotgun I kept under my bed was in place before I went to sleep.

I had to reach for it late at night, about a year later, when there was a loud banging on the door of the metal-framed room that had been affixed to the small caravan in which I slept.

"Boss! Boss! Boss!" I heard. "Come out!"

Opening the door, I was confronted by a mob with flaming torches. They were agitated as their story spilled out. A man had been caught molesting one of the boys in the laborers' village at the edge of our camp. A swarm of people had beaten him and tied him up, and those who raced to my door were worried he would be summarily executed.

Reading the mood, I sensed that, if I didn't act fast, it was going to be too late to stop the vigilante justice. I grabbed the shotgun from under my bed, called a couple of my white field assistants out from their beds, and we marched down to the village where the man was being held. He was bleeding from the severe beating.

With people around me shouting and waving their arms, I announced as confidently as I could that I was arresting him—even though I had no real authority to do so. We pulled him out and marched him back to the main camp, where we locked him in a storage shed and kept him safe under armed guard until I could have him escorted to Grootfontein—and the nearest police station—the next day.

Incidents like this taught me the importance of being decisive. I found that I had an aptitude for reading people, organizing, and leading. It was seat-of-the-pants, not textbook, but it worked.

A big factor was my "management by walking around." I'd read about it somewhere and decided to put it into practice. I found that being visible and friendly somehow made being firm easier; I wasn't some remote figure who just came out of an office somewhere to bark an order.

I'd stroll down to the laborers' camp, where the most senior workers were allowed to bring their families. The children would be running around as their mothers cooked over open fires outside their basic, galvanized-iron huts. I'd ask questions, using a combination of sign language and my limited Afrikaans.

The conversations were a bit stilted, but I sensed that people appreciated the effort I was making and that I wasn't just stuck behind my desk only talking to people who understood English. This feeling was later affirmed when someone let slip the tribal nickname I had been given. Assigned to all outsiders, these titles describing the essential personality or characteristics of the individual were a fiercely guarded secret among the workers.

Mine, I discovered, translated to, "He who comes, sees, and walks away."

The shotgun earned me some respect—not because they feared me using it against them but because they wanted me to use it on snakes. I discovered that they were absolutely terrified of snakes, so whenever one was spotted slithering around, I was called on to come and dispatch it.

I made some small efforts to challenge the prevailing racial prejudice. I got permission to promote two of my brightest African workers to field assistants—a position traditionally reserved for whites. To me it was simply a matter of good sense: one of them, Pedro, spoke half a dozen languages fluently, including Latin. He was far more educated than I was. Why on earth would I not use his abilities as much as possible?

I wasn't looking to start a revolution, just trying to do my job as well as possible.

I was also enjoying the beauty of that largely untouched, unexplored part of the world. In my spare time, I'd take one of the company 4x4s—always making sure that it was in good working order, had a spare tire (two, preferably), parts, and was stocked with plenty of water—and explore the area. We had no radios in the vehicles, and you wouldn't want to find yourself stranded out there.

Once some of my team found two guys out in the Kalahari, the vast, semiarid thornbush plains stretching across South-

West Africa, South Africa, and Botswana. We were doing some exploratory work there when they came across two men who came staggering out of nowhere. They'd been stuck in the desert for several days, had drunk all the radiator fluid from their vehicle to try to stay hydrated, and were close to death. We gave them tiny sips of water and soup before getting them to the nearest hospital.

Despite the danger, I was drawn to explore the openness. The vaulted open skies and the fabulous feeling of freedom thrilled me. This was untouched reality, not some tamed game park. But it was safe enough if you were responsible. On overnight trips, I'd sometimes just sleep on the ground beside the jeep. Being something of an introvert, it was rejuvenating to be out there in the bush alone, knowing that there was not another soul for miles and miles around.

Some way south of Tsumkwe was a series of pans, or shallow lakes, that attracted a dazzling array of birds. There were yellow-billed hornbills, whose swoopy flight made them seem half drunk. Iridescent starlings. Lilac-breasted rollers. I had a book detailing all the different species and would check them off as I spotted them.

Then there was the larger wildlife: antelope, impala, springboks, kudu, hunting dogs, giraffes, and lions. One time when driving out to where we were drilling, I rounded a bend and had to slam on the brakes as I found myself speeding toward a big herd of elephants. I quickly threw the vehicle into reverse and got out of there since the two cardinal rules of being out in the open were don't startle the animals and don't make them feel cornered.

THEN I MET JOHN. I came across him on a trip into Tsumkwe and was surprised to see his white face there. The handful of whites in town included a doctor and the guy responsible for the conservation area. John, it turned out, was an American filmmaker camping nearby with his English girlfriend. I began to visit them on Saturday evenings, and we'd sit around the campfire and chat. He was in his fifties, while she was considerably younger. They seemed intriguingly adventurous to me, almost bohemian, and I was fascinated to learn why they were out in that remote part of the continent.

John was continuing his family's work with the Bushmen, the famed nomadic stone-age hunter-gatherers who had roamed the Kalahari for centuries. With their lighter skin, they were notably different from the other, darker tribal groups in South-West Africa that generally looked down on them.

Sometime in the late 1960s, the government had decided it should help the Bushmen settle down, creating concrete-home villages like Tsumkwe. Like many such enterprises, this effort may have been well intended, but it was hopelessly unhelpful. Dislocated from their traditional way of life, the Bushmen struggled to adapt to their new, settled circumstances. Cut off from their heritage, most had trouble finding work. Diseases like tuberculosis became rampant, and alcoholism was common. Many committed suicide.

John's father, a sociologist and filmmaker, had traveled to Africa to study the Bushmen in the fifties, and now John was following in his footsteps. He was making a documentary to bring the plight of the Bushmen to public attention to see if something could be done to help them.

As John explained the Bushmen's circumstances, a sense of indignation rose up in me on their behalf. It was as though John had lit a fuse in me, igniting something deep inside—something that went back to my childhood. A buried anger at injustice.

Things hadn't been easy growing up. I first became aware that all wasn't quite right between my mum and my dad when I was about three or four. The air of tension in the home grew. I'd sit at the top of the stairs with my sister, Jan, and we'd listen to the raised voices downstairs, fearing there might be raised hands too. Dad began spending more and more time away from home, and when he was there, he might as well have not been. He left the first time when I was around eight, and then, when I was about thirteen, he left for good.

As our home fell apart, I resented having to take on responsibilities that I knew were beyond my years. As the oldest child, I found myself being drawn into the role of mediator, negotiating visiting rights between my parents. My mother would sometimes talk with me about her financial worries. It felt like I was the only man in the family trying to hold things together. It all made me very angry, resulting in repeated problems at school. I'd get into fights and end up in the headmaster's study for another caning. That just made me even angrier, creating an ongoing spiral.

Then came the day I was caught shoplifting. Mum called Dad to tell him what had happened, and he came to the house to deliver the punishment. What hurt most was the overwhelming sense of the unjustness of it all. How hypocritical, it seemed to me, that he could cause all sorts of chaos, come and chastise me for reacting poorly to what he had done, and then just leave again.

Something of this deep-seated dissatisfaction with the way things were was reawakened in me as John talked about the Bushmen. What they had experienced was terrible. Something needed to be done. And I realized that maybe this time I could be the one to do something about it. I was no longer a kid who just had to suck it up. I actually had some clout I could use.

John penned a couple of letters to some of the authorities who oversaw things in the province, urging them to investigate conditions and affect some changes. He asked me to be a cosignatory, and I agreed willingly. Not long after, I got a visit from a couple of South African secret police. They'd learned that I was stirring things up, they told me, and it was in my best interests not to rock the boat anymore if I didn't want to be expelled.

I decided on more direct action. Meaningful employment would help, I realized, so I tried to think of a way of creating jobs for the Bushmen. It occurred to me that, instead of using a bulldozer to cut the rudimentary roads we had to make through the bush, I could employ the local Bushmen. The pidgin Afrikaans I had learned to communicate with my workers at the exploration sites was no good with the

Bushmen, so John served as my translator when I met with the local elders.

Rather than spend money on a bulldozer, I explained that I wanted to pay them to cut a way through the bush for me. It was the first time any Bushmen had been employed by any commercial company outside of working on the farms. And though I did not realize it at the time, it was also my first effort at development—and one that would foreshadow the lesson to come: solutions are often not as easy as they first seem.

One thing I hadn't allowed for when hiring the Bushmen was the fact that, with a heritage of wandering hardwired into their character, they did not grasp the concept of regular work hours—the nine-to-five thing. If they decided it was a good day to go hunting, some of them would go, without letting anyone know. So I hired the elders to manage the job. I told them, "I will pay you so much for every kilometer of road you cut for me. I'll give you the money, and it's up to you to see that the task is accomplished and that the money is distributed in the best way. You know your people, and you know what works."

I didn't realize how significant my time in Africa had been until my mum and Jan came out to visit. We vacationed in Pietermaritzburg, South Africa, and it was almost like old times; we'd traveled in Europe quite a lot when I was young. Those trips had instilled in me a fascination with new places and people who were different.

A waiter who almost turned ineptitude into an art form served us one night while we dined in South Africa. He was hopeless, forgetting to take part of an order and then bringing the wrong thing. I'd take a deep breath, point out what was wrong, and ask him if he wouldn't mind fixing it, and somehow we made it through the meal.

"You know, Doug, you've really changed," Mum said later. "In the past, you'd have blown a gasket with him or with me or someone! What's happened?"

I was learning to channel anger into positive change.

LEARNING THE SYSTEMS

I DIDN'T REALIZE IT AT THE TIME, but I returned from Namibia with two new passions that would intertwine and shape the course of the rest of my life—as well as an undetected high level of stress.

Being responsible for running things in an essentially lawless place with the threat of violence never far away had quietly set my inner vigilance meter on high. This only became apparent when I was on vacation in the Lake District, a beautiful hill-walking region in the north of England. Shopping in a supermarket one day, I dropped to the floor at what I thought to be the sudden sound of gunfire. Customers looked at me a bit oddly as I sheepishly got to my feet after realizing the noise had been caused by a tumbling stack of canned goods.

I'd come back home, in part, to learn how to trump the accountants. During two and a half years in South-West Africa, I'd been given increasing responsibility with De Beers, overseeing searches for new diamond fields. But senior management listened to the bean counters and kept overruling my geologist recommendations. I realized that I didn't have enough financial language to speak persuasively.

I also wanted to learn more about running organizations. I hadn't set out to be a leader but had found myself in the role. I also discovered I had an aptitude for leading others and enjoyed the challenge of focusing people on a goal.

My middle-management experience earned me a spot as the second-youngest student in an intensive, one-year MBA course. Most of the 150 or so other students were midcareer, middle-management types looking to improve their promotion prospects. My plan was to gain some more management skills and then take them to western Australia, where diamonds had recently been discovered.

But I couldn't shake the questions that had been raised by my involvement with the Bushmen. I hadn't set out to hurt anyone when I headed to Africa—the dream of adventure and girls just seemed much more appealing than the get-by job I'd had driving deliveries around London construction sites since graduating. I didn't consider myself to be a prejudiced person, and I'd actually tried to help the people around me in Tsumkwe and Sigeriti as best I could. But I began to wonder about the morality of what I had been involved in. I decided that my MBA thesis should attempt to evaluate the impact of De Beers's presence in South-West Africa.

I loved and hated the MBA program. It was hugely demanding; other than giving myself each Friday night off, it was all work. We were split into groups that were assigned a biweekly business case study to complete over the weekend. My group included a self-made businessman who'd turned scrap metal into a successful company and an investment banker. It was fascinating to hear their different perspectives and ideas.

I was excited to learn about finance and accounting, filling in a sorely missing piece of my knowledge base. And while I also discovered new things about management and leadership, what was especially encouraging was that much of what I heard and read confirmed so many of the things I had been doing and the way I had operated intuitively while in Africa.

Delegation was one area. I saw how my natural ability to read people had helped me know when to be directive and when to give people more freedom. Some guys could only be trusted to complete a task well if every step was spelled out, like Nathaniel, my cook. He was eager to serve, but I soon discovered he had to be guided every step of the way. Others had thrived when I told them what needed to be done and pretty much left them to it.

From my MBA studies, I also gained the language I needed to better understand organizational development, how systems work, and why, sometimes, they don't. In learning more about managing people, business processes, and organizational development, I was being given a framework for all that I had experienced.

In the same way that, for me, geology had always been about more than looking at rocks—it was part of a bigger way of looking at the world and why things were the way they were—organizational design came alive. Organizations were more than just a group of people, products, and processes but were sometimes a mysterious combination of all three. How people worked and how they worked together intrigued me.

One of the things that became clear was the marked difference between leadership and management, yet the two are often linked as though they are the same thing. My MBA studies helped me begin to see the distinction.

Leadership is about having a vision, knowing where to go, creating a sense of momentum, and providing the forward movement. Management is about the details and getting there the best way. Typically the problems come when you have a big-picture, visionary leader trying to manage the nuts and bolts, or vice versa. Yet as I studied and reflected, I realized that somehow I seemed to have the ability to hold both in tension. I loved thinking big and wrestling with abstract ideas, but I also enjoyed systems and efficiency.

Seeing both sides like this enhanced my thesis assessment of De Beers and my time in South-West Africa. For me, there was no completely clear-cut answer. Critics argued that De Beers and others like them were simply exploitative, supporting—even indirectly—a semi-apartheid system and ransacking the country's wealth. Yet as I studied financial reports, I saw that the business was creating jobs and paying taxes that helped the government provide things like roads and schooling.

Above all, I recognized that we live in an inextricably interrelated world and that some day, in some way, I wanted to be part of bringing positive change on a bigger scale than I had done with the Bushmen. As part of our MBA studies, we completed a series of personality-profile tests and career-guidance questionnaires to help us look to the future. I wrote down two dreams: to manage my own business consultancy and to be involved in international development.

That was all sometime in the future, however. Meanwhile, I needed a job. Toward the end of my MBA course, I was presented with a great one. The mining director of a major De Beers rival offered me a position as his personal assistant. I'd get to travel the world, visiting and assessing the company's mining operations. This prospect was much more like my girls-and-fast-cars idea of geology than living in a caravan out in the African bush had been.

There was one complication, however. Her name was Anna.

WE MET ON A HIKING WEEKEND organized in North Wales by mutual friends. There were about a dozen of us. I spotted her during the first evening get-together. I'd heard she was a psychologist doing postgraduate studies and thought that her conservative appearance probably indicated a demure and passive approach to life.

I had to revise my hasty evaluation of her the next morning when we all set off to drive to the starting point for our walk. I got into Anna's car and was impressed by how she took the wheel: strong, confident, and more like a guy than most women motorists I'd observed. As someone who loves cars, I liked this. There was something quite appealing about her.

Wrapped up well against the spring chill, we spent the day together, walking, talking, and laughing our way up and then down the three thousand feet of Snowdon. Too caught up in our conversation, I didn't take in much of the scenery. She was very easy to talk to, and very quickly our conversation moved from superficial topics to a deeper sharing of our own experiences. We told each other about our families. I heard about her work helping people with problems. I recounted some of my experiences in Africa, and she told me about her travels in Mexico. As we exchanged stories and insights, we realized that our perspectives on the world were similar due to our shared faith in God. The time seemed to fly by.

When I was offered the international mining job a few months later, I knew that it meant choosing between it and Anna. The position was really appealing—pretty much a dream job for a man in his early twenties. Travel the world and find precious metals; it seemed like a real-life version of the fictional geologists I had read about. Very tempting, but I decided that, by staying home, I could check two of the lures off my private wish list: a great girl—and one who liked fast cars. I made the right choice.

Now I had to find a different job. Through a friend, I interviewed for a position as a mining analyst with a London stockbroker's firm. They decided not to fill that position, but they did offer me one as a retail analyst. I didn't know much about shopping, except that I found it pretty boring, but I had an MBA loan to pay off, and the opportunity meant a salary, so I said yes.

My time at the London Stock Exchange in an office above the famous trading floor was an eye-opener. First I learned that a fancy MBA didn't mean too much to most people in the real business world. The partner I reported to repeatedly bled critical red ink over my early reports. It was painful and humbling, but she taught me how to write concisely and clearly.

As I studied the retail sector, I began to see it with different eyes, in much the same way I'd discovered a new dimension through geology. Curious to see what was selling, how it was selling it, and to whom, I dragged Anna into clothes stores, rather than the other way around, when out shopping.

Thrown into analyzing a commercial world about which I had no knowledge, I learned the importance of asking lots of questions. The latest fashions didn't just end up on the shelves by accident. They arrived there as the result of a complex blend of design seasons, manufacturing cycles, and supply-chain sequences. I began to understand how systems worked and fit together.

At the same time, I was surprised by how fickle the financial markets were; despite all the analysis and deliberation, people could still end up making trading decisions almost seemingly on a whim or because of a short-lived rumor.

This was also my first experience of meeting senior businesspeople. I may have still been young and comparatively inexperienced, but I had exposure to some of the top level of Britain's business community—lots of household names. I learned a lot about how these influential people handled themselves and how they operated. On the positive side, I absorbed their thoughts and ideas about the development of business strategy and processes. The negative behaviors I saw of those who obviously felt very superior and the demoralizing and sometimes demeaning way these managers treated others impressed me less.

My stockbroker work underscored the importance of asking the right questions. Our analyses were based not only on reading companies' annual reports and dissecting their financial statements but also carefully matching them against the answers we got. I learned how important it was to prepare in advance, as we would usually have only a short amount of time with these senior business leaders to learn all that we needed to make our recommendations. So we spent a lot of time preparing the questions we would ask.

Though the job was giving me lots of valuable experience, I knew it wasn't a long-term fit. I was growing increasingly uncomfortable with the whole culture, especially with its emphasis on image, pretension, and shallow, slick self-promotion. I wasn't opposed to people doing well financially, but it seemed to me that there had to be more to life than just that.

After Anna and I got married, we rented a little cottage near Wallingford, a pretty, historic market town not far from Oxford. It was convenient for Anna, close to where she was working for the National Health Service, but it meant quite a commute to London for me. On top of the long office hours, the travel meant that, as newlyweds, Anna and I only saw each other mostly on the weekends. When she was offered a new position in Bromsgrove, even farther from London, we decided enough was enough. I resigned from stockbroking and became a kept man.

After three months of applying for jobs in our new area and getting nowhere, I was feeling pretty discouraged. Then Anna pulled from the trash can a job ad I had looked at and discarded. It was for a position with something to do with computer-aided design, manufacturing, and systems engineering—about which I knew nothing.

"You should apply," Anna told me. "You never know."

And so I joined what turned out to be an internal-management consultancy for one of Britain's largest manufacturing and engineering businesses. Lucas Engineering & Systems had been set up to help breathe new life into Lucas Industries. Producing components for a wide range of businesses across the aerospace, automotive, and applied technology industries, the company was struggling mightily in the face of Japanese competition. Things just had to change.

John Parnaby—Lucas's manufacturing director, who was a creative, out-of-the-box thinker with some radical ideas about restructuring and reorganization—was spearheading the effort. He was building an internal consultancy team tasked with bringing about big results, and the company offered me a spot.

THE CONSULTANCY WORK taught me the importance of diplomacy. It's not enough to come up with good recommendations; you have to be able to convince people of the value of those solutions. After all, they are the ones who are going to implement your ideas and see them succeed or fail. Though we were an internal unit within the broader business, our services weren't forced on any of the individual Lucas general managers. First we had to persuade them that we could help and then show them how.

In fact, it would have been easier if we had been outsiders. External consultants have a certain measure of authority because senior management has brought them in, whereas we were viewed with a level of suspicion because we were part of the company but independent in a sense, too. That didn't always make us very popular—particularly in the beginning.

But it was clear that the business needed overhauling. New technology presented great opportunities but also created challenges. You couldn't just swap out one part of the overall operation without affecting other areas as well. You had to rethink the rest of the system, stripping things down to their basics and rebuilding.

Changing production meant redesigning the factory. That would require reexamining the supply chain, which in turn necessitated looking closely at financial procedures. Research and development and marketing would also need to be reviewed and maybe retooled. Everything was interconnected.

Evaluating all this required more than just management input. I soon found out that, if you want to know how to change a business, you should ask the people at the operational end on the factory floor. They are watching what goes on day in and day out, yet many times they are overlooked and often never consulted. As we took on consultancy projects, we would create teams not only of executives but also representatives from the workforce. I'd be the external facilitator, drawing out their differing insights, and they would find a way to piece them all together.

Some fixes were fairly obvious, making me wonder why they'd never been made before. Like the small-business unit that had three different cafeterias for a group that was only a hundred or so strong, with one a fancy silver service for management only. Not only was that a waste of money, the elitist style also undermined company morale. But recommending its closure did not make me welcome in some circles.

Aware that the executives to whom I was reporting were often twenty years my senior, I knew that I'd have to work hard to overcome some understandable resistance and resentment. What did someone in his midtwenties know about anything?

Thankfully, the results of our systematic attention to data, metrics, and performance seemed to speak for themselves. Our unit scored a number of successes that caught people's attention. After a couple of years, someone from one of the Lucas divisions where I'd led a consultancy review asked if I wanted to become the new materials manager there.

Though it gave me a whole new level of experience, I might not have accepted the position if I had known what was ahead. I was responsible for the materials, supplies, and quality of production across three auto-lighting factories with around 1,200 employees.

I have been in many demanding situations since, but those twelve months were probably the single-most extended period of stress I have ever known. Every day consisted of putting out new fires that had ignited overnight.

A car headlamp seems a pretty basic thing until you're the one responsible for having all the thirty or more parts needed to make one there at the same time—both the pieces you manufacture and others that come from external suppliers with their own logistical headaches. Suddenly it feels like you are one of those Rollerblading plate spinners at the circus.

The afternoon status meetings were dreadful. All the bucks seemed to stop at my desk. We'd discover that one small component was missing, perhaps because it had been misidentified, which slowed or halted the production line. Then there'd be a call from Ford's purchasing director, who complained that our delays in production had stopped his company's vehicle assembly lines and were costing them millions of pounds as they idled, and what was I going to do about it?

There would be all-night sessions to try to get things back on track. On occasion, we'd even rush a delivery of badly needed parts by taxi, just to keep assembly going. I learned a lot during that high-pressure assignment, and it gave me a deeper appreciation for the stress some people face in trying to deliver required results. But I wasn't too sad when the division was sold off and I returned to the internal consultancy.

By this time, what we had achieved had earned some outside interest, and other companies requested our services. Having always been fascinated by marketing, I was appointed sales and marketing manager for the unit, which had grown to around two hundred strong. The increase in personnel was only one indicator of how well our work had gone. More sobering was the workforce reduction across Lucas as some of our recommendations were implemented. Hard decisions had to be made for the business to survive.

Recognizing that our systems approach was transferable, we began working in different industries. Tracking parts in manufacturing could be translated into other areas, like banking. We consulted with banks that were looking to develop their cash-center and check-processing services and began discussions with some of the players in oil exploration to see how we might help them.

The work was challenging but great. I was enjoying the rewards, too: a nice company car and a good, senior manager's salary with a comfortable pension plan. Anna and I had bought our first home and were expecting our first baby. Everything was going well, but there was a nagging sense of something missing, like an itch just out of reach. We were restless. As we looked ahead to the next twenty or thirty years on my career track, it all seemed somewhat predictable. We both needed there to be something more.

Anna and I had settled in at a local church, made friends, and gotten involved in congregational life. We were happy enough but talked together about whether we might bring our work lives and our faith more into alignment somehow. There was a big world out there, and we wanted to be part of making a difference—somehow.

We thought our skills and experiences might be of interest to some Christian-based organizations involved in international projects. We contacted a number of them, and the response was disappointing. They weren't really interested in our professional backgrounds and suggested we go to Bible college. That idea just didn't click with us.

We were pretty discouraged by the time we went to a weeklong Christian conference with some friends from church. One of the speakers piqued our interest, though. He talked about the work of Youth With A Mission, where he was one of the leaders. Sounding a bit like a Christian version of the Peace Corps, this volunteer organization was involved in a wide range of innovative programs around the world.

Anna and I stayed to speak with the presenter after one of his sessions and told him about our interest in doing something different from the nine-to-five life we were locked in. He was enthusiastic, explaining how his group needed all kinds of professionals. He mentioned there being a place for psychologists, and Anna smiled. Then he mentioned the need for managers and MBAs, and I knew what was next for us.

John Parnaby was surprised when I thanked him for the opportunity of being part of his Lucas team and handed in my notice. He praised my work and pointed out the benefits I was enjoying. Why was I leaving?

"Well, fundamentally, I want to make a difference in the world in some way," I told him. "I want to do something more."

LOOKING FOR MORE

CLASSROOMS AND BOARDROOMS had given me business and management skills, but I discovered how I wanted to apply them while I was on the streets of Bogota, Colombia.

Anna and I went there with our firstborn, daughter Alex, as part of a volunteer Youth With A Mission team. We'd spent three months studying and team building in Amsterdam, preparing to work alongside another group in the organization that was running projects to help Colombian street kids.

Like many other countries in South America, Africa, and Asia, Colombia had a growing population of abandoned and runaway children on its city streets. The victims of abuse, neglect, or just grinding poverty, these homeless youngsters typically congregated in small gangs, getting by on begging and crime.

Street kids are a mercurial mix: needy children at heart— some as young as five or six—and yet sadly wise beyond their years. They can flip between these two extremes in an instant, making efforts to befriend them and earn their trust challenging.

What made the work in Bogota even more difficult was that the Colombian capital was then the center of an increasingly violent struggle between the authorities and the country's powerful drug cartels. We'd often hear bomb blasts or be told of police who had been murdered on the street as we made our way around some of the rougher parts of the city where the kids would gather. And we stood out a bit—a tall white guy and his wife pushing a stroller with a thirteen-month-old in it. But our strangeness seemed appealing to some of the kids, and we were able to strike up some friendships with our pidgin Spanish and free hot chocolate and bread.

Our job was to try to be a first point of contact. At night we would go out to meet specific street gangs under a bridge or in a city-center location and befriend the kids. When we connected with some of them, we'd then invite them to a drop-in center the organization ran. There they could get a shower, some food, basic medical attention, and, perhaps most importantly, some adult concern. It was all very low-key and open door; the skittish visitors were free to leave at any time.

Those who came to trust some of the workers were then given the opportunity to stay at a slightly more structured halfway house in another part of the city. From there, those who really wanted to make a break from the streets could move to a farm out in the country, where they could pick up their education, get some job skills, and maybe even be reunited with their families.

It was slow, often unrewarding work. Many kids would take a handout, but they didn't want a hand up. They were suspicious of adults and especially wary of anyone official; death squads, some believed to comprise police officers, were known to "clean up" parts of the city from time to time. We'd be sitting with a group of street kids, chatting and playing, when they would suddenly jump up and disappear because someone in uniform had come into view.

Sleeping under bridges or in abandoned buildings, these youngsters were unsure where their next meal would come from, yet they were often reluctant to leave the relative familiarity of the streets for an unknown alternative. Violence and ubiquitous glue sniffing only dampened their desire for change. It was distressing and disheartening to see how quickly they became hardened. Even in the few months we were in Colombia, we saw new arrivals on the street soon become numbed and distrustful.

Watching these dirty, jumpy, suspicious kids play innocently with Alex, I couldn't help but be moved by their plight. Yes, many of them were violent and dangerous, but the odds had been stacked against them by an uncaring society. It stirred and fanned the embers of my deep-seated sense of injustice, which had first been lit by my own childhood experiences and further fueled by the African Bushmen. What was happening on the streets of Bogota and countless other cities around the world wasn't right. The children deserved more. They deserved what Alex received: protection and provision, attention and affection, and nourishment and nurture.

At the same time, I recognized that I wasn't particularly gifted for working with them directly. I cared, and I was concerned, but I didn't see myself being especially effective, long-term, as a field—or street—worker. But in the weeks we spent in Bogota, I came to know without a shadow of a doubt that I wanted to give the rest of my life to helping to recruit, equip, and enable others much better suited and qualified to take my place.

Having had the opportunity to make some organizational recommendations to the leaders of the Bogota project to help increase their impact, we returned to Amsterdam to join Youth With A Mission full-time. Over the next couple of years, I helped leaders of the group's wide-ranging programs in the Dutch city complete an organizational review and restructuring, and I consulted with the movement's national leaders back in England.

Even more fulfilling for me was to be asked to offer organizational counsel to Youth With A Mission leaders in Africa, taking me back to the continent for the first time since I had quit De Beers. Many of the organization's initiatives there involved relief and development services in some way, further stirring my desire to help those in need.

I also linked up with leaders of the organization heading development efforts in other parts of the world. We began discussing ways we might foster more collaboration, communication, and consistency in some of those endeavors.

It felt like everything was coming together. I was excited to be able to bring my professional skills to bear on a personal conviction that some people get shortchanged by life and that the rest of us have an obligation—a duty, if you will—to help redress some of that imbalance. Feelings weren't enough, though. It was a matter of bringing head and heart together.

I knew that I needed more firsthand experience of the realities of doing so. The opportunity came in 1991, in what we thought was the aftermath of the Liberian civil war. Anna and I were asked to lead a multinational team formed by Medair, a Swiss-based crisis-relief organization affiliated with Youth With A Mission, to help meet some of the dire social and medical needs resulting from the ugly conflict.

Liberia was, in many ways, a proving ground. Our time there didn't just make me face my own mortality during the hours of my arrest at gunpoint. It also dispelled any vaguely romantic notions I may have had about doing good; you might say I swapped rose-colored glasses for twenty-twenty lenses.

During our year with the Medair program, I met some remarkable people. They were doing incredible work at great personal sacrifice. But I also saw how exposure to suffering and injustice on such a scale can lead to cynicism and suspicion. Some in the larger international-relief community we were part of coped with the strain by drinking or having indiscriminate relationships. Members of our own team struggled with personal issues raised by being in the center of such an extreme situation.

Then there was the indifference and sometimes-outright hostility from those we were seeking to help. I didn't expect or want people to feel beholden to us, but it was gratifying to hear the occasional thanks—to be reminded tangibly and personally that we were making a difference. Being accused of self-interest, of only being there because we were making a lot of money out of other people's misfortune, could be hard.

But the imperfections of both the helpers and the helped didn't dampen my desire to be involved. It just made me more determined that, given the cost, any investment in doing good should make as big a return as possible.

ANOTHER DISREGARDED NEWSPAPER AD provided the opportunity to begin working out how to marry a sense of mission with some way to measure its success.

After de-stressing on our return to England, we watched for news on television as our remaining team was forced to flee the country a few months after our departure, when Liberia descended into civil war chaos once more.

I'd sought opportunities with a number of different relief and development organizations back in the United Kingdom, but no doors had opened. That's how I found myself working again as a business consultant. When no charity job came up, I'd contacted people at Lucas, my former employer, to see if they might have some part-time work for me.

The new guy in charge invited me in to chat. He said he'd heard about what I had done while I was there and offered me my former boss's job. So for the next two years, I was back in the world of systems reengineering and reorganization. As a Lucas director, I found myself traveling and consulting with outside clients, including some leading banks. It was fairly big-league business, but I couldn't shake the feeling that I really should be doing more with my life.

Then a friend began nagging me about a job she had seen advertised. Tearfund was looking for a new CEO. Founded in 1972 and supported mostly by individual churchgoers who wanted to express their Christian beliefs by funding practical acts of care, Tearfund had grown to become the sixth-largest aid agency of any kind, faith-based or not, in the country.

The job seemed to be beyond my resume, so I dismissed it. But my friend wouldn't let it go, kind of like when Anna had dug that Lucas ad out of the trash years before. To get my friend off my back, I completed the application form.

I was surprised when told soon thereafter that I'd been short-listed for the post—and even more taken aback then to be finally offered the job.

If my experiences in South-West Africa, Bogota, and Liberia had been formative, the almost ten years I spent at Tearfund were foundational. My encounters with the Bushmen, the street kids, and the child soldiers created the mold, and heading Tearfund pressed my molten materials into shape.

In the business world, my job had been to bring health to ailing endeavors or, as gently and graciously as possible, recommend withdrawing life support. That wasn't the problem at Tearfund, which was widely recognized for the good work it did. Around two hundred staff in the United Kingdom and double that number overseas successfully facilitated a wide range of programs—from farming and health to education and disaster relief—in more than one hundred countries. The question was, "How could we do even more?"

To achieve that goal, some things did need to change; that was clear. Tearfund's donor base was aging, and a transfusion of fresh blood was vital. Then there was the question of positioning. With a firmly and unapologetically faith-based dimension to its work—all grants went to local church- or other Christian-based programs—Tearfund stood apart from the wider, general relief-and-development community. I appreciated the mission focus but felt that need not be lost in being more open to interacting with other agencies from which we might learn and, in turn, be able to positively impact. We did good work, I reasoned, and need not fear scrutiny from others.

As I looked more closely at the organization, I realized that Tearfund was like a plant that needed repotting. It had grown about as much as it could in its current shape and form. Restructuring was a gradual process, continuing the good work while making internal changes that would enable us to do even more.

After five years, we had reorganized and rebranded, broadening our support base without losing the longtime constituency, and doubled our income along the way. We had also instituted a more rigorous internal-evaluation process by which we estimated that we were seeing three times the impact with twice the money. We were doing more, better.

But as I traveled to scores of countries, seeing remarkable projects firsthand, I became increasingly aware that just doing our thing better wasn't enough. I felt like a photographer moving from shooting portraits to landscapes. Rather than just focusing on having a really clear, close-up image of what we were involved in, we needed to zoom out with a wider lens and see the bigger picture. We could feed the hungry, keeping them alive. But what about the circumstances that left them without food in the first place, like war, poor business practices, or corruption?

Without an optimal environment—social, cultural, environmental, religious, political, economic, and more—the best efforts will only go so far. Without the best context, good content can only achieve so much, and it's doomed to a repetitive cycle. It's only ever treating the symptoms, never trying to eradicate the disease. It's one thing to help the poor, but it's another to try to understand and change the circumstances that have made them poor.

I began carrying a trilevel *Star Trek* chess set to Tearfund meetings to use it as a visual aid for talking about how we needed to look at change three-dimensionally. The three tier set over which Spock would muse in the television series perfectly illustrated, for me, how complicated development work is. I explained that those three levels represented the international, national, and local dynamics at play in each situation, some more obvious than others.

The *Star Trek* board also helped me show how bottom-up and top-down strategies have to be aligned. For Tearfund, that meant embracing the idea of advocacy, both nationally and internationally. Up to that point, the emphasis had been on action—doing things. Calling for change from those in power was a new way of looking at our work.

We began small, lending our voice to an embryonic, turn-of-the-millennium campaign that called on the leading Group of Eight nations to forgive the massive unpayable debts dating back more than twenty years and crippling so many developing countries. Some in Tearfund were concerned that many of our longtime donors might be offended by this move into what looked like political activism, reaching out and linking with other groups, including trade unions, for the first time.

But many Tearfund supporters, including my family (now supplemented by Ryan, our five year-old), were among the sixty thousand people who formed a human chain around the G8 leaders' venue in Birmingham, England, in May 1998 and urged them to drop the debts.

Through this campaign, we learned that, as an organization, we could work together with others for the greater good while retaining our distinctiveness. And I saw that this kind of scale could produce results: the action we were part of was a factor in the G8's subsequent slashing of developing-world debt. In turn, that meant, in Uganda, for example, government money once lost to repaying loans could be put into education. School enrollment mushroomed as a result, promising further long-term community benefits.

IF THE FIRST HALF OF MY TENURE at Tearfund centered on maximizing the organization's efforts, the second became about multiplying them. I was pleased with all that we had achieved in improving and increasing our results, but it still wasn't enough for me. No matter how good we became, I knew that we weren't going to be sufficient on our own. I wanted to find out how we might broaden and deepen Tearfund's impact beyond just our own efforts.

The first tentative step in that direction was the formation of the Micah Network, which was initiated by and through members of the international Tearfund network and comprised groups in other countries that shared the Tearfund name but were organizationally and operationally independent. The Micah Network brought together Western and non-Western Christian aid organizations in an informal community intended to provide a place where they could learn from, encourage, and even collaborate with each other.

Western groups had plenty of opportunities to access this kind of forum, but it was much harder for people from other parts of the world. And when they did manage to attend events, they tended to be Western top-heavy. The others needed their own place and space, and bringing them together also gave their part of the world a louder collective voice.

Today more than five hundred organizations participate in workshops, forums, and consultations intended to foster learning and practices and share resources, research, and information as part of the Micah Network.

This was just one of the *Star Trek* chess levels I envisaged; however, I felt that a truly effective strategy had to take into account more than just networking and capacity building. Action on the ground, the kind of programs all our different organizations were involved in, was one, of course. The other was advocacy.

So next was the Micah Challenge, again established with Tearfund network support. This initiative was intended to help give the worldwide church a global voice on poverty by educating and training Christians on how they could be actively involved in issues of poverty and injustice. It was particularly focused around the recently agreed upon Millennium Development Goals.

Established at a United Nations' summit marking the start of the third millennium, these ambitious goals included eradicating extreme poverty and hunger, reducing child mortality, improving maternal health, ensuring universal primary education, and combating major diseases like AIDS and malaria.

Bringing different organizations together around even such universally accepted objectives took a lot of time and patience. After four years of networking of this kind, it became clear that my days at Tearfund were drawing to a close for a couple of reasons.

On a practical level, I was nearing the ten years I'd always seen as the optimum term for the leader of a large organization. There are exceptions, but generally this seems to be the span of their greatest effectiveness. I have observed that, more often than not, after this amount of time, the leader tends to get too familiar, too confident, and starts taking the board for granted—who, in turn, think it's time to find fresh vision. Also, I'd encouraged Tearfund through about as much change as I could.

Additionally, I wanted to see if I could take the collaborative approach I'd been advocating to Tearfund and other organizations a step further. So in due course, I stepped down from Tearfund to formally launch Integral, an international association of faith-based relief organizations.

This was another step in my journey toward maximizing charitable impact. The Micah Network had been the first attempt to look beyond an individual organization's efforts. Bringing like-minded groups together in an informal community to share ideas and resources made the least demands on those participating. The Micah Challenge took things a bit further, with members giving not just a certain amount of their time but also money to shared goals—in this case, advocacy efforts. Participants had more skin in the game, as it were.

But I felt that there were still ways in which kindred organizations could do more cooperatively. In founding Integral, I believed that, by agreeing to work together on the ground, these organizations could multiply their collective efforts without compromising their individual identities or revenue streams.

For example, they could collaborate on gathering and sharing marketing and media resources. And with agreed protocols, they could work more efficiently in crisis situations, offering one combined reference point to government and other international-aid agencies.

Even with agreement on the goals and goodwill, it wasn't easy to turn the theory into reality. The twenty or so national agencies I first invited to be part of this initiative had different mission statements and operating guidelines. And there was some genuine concern about giving up their autonomy.

But eventually Integral launched with thirteen founding member organizations committed to working together more collaboratively in the pursuit of greater impact. I was excited but already looking further down the road: what if, rather than just agreeing to work together more effectively on their existing programs, Integral members looked for a project they might initiate together?

That's what I was working on when I got an unexpected call from Steve Beck, the senior vice president of Geneva Global. I had first connected with Steve when I was still at Tearfund, and he had contacted me to know more about our work with community-based groups for the philanthropic organization he was leading in the United States.

A couple of years after that initial call, we met up when I spent some time on sabbatical in America. Deep into my thinking about how to achieve greater impact by bringing development organizations together more, I spent several weeks studying networking, alliances, and organizational collaboration at Eastern University in St. Davids, Pennsylvania.

Steve had discovered I was there and made contact. He invited me to visit his organization based in nearby Radnor and speak to the staff about my work and what I had learned about effective international development. Impressed by the enthusiastic and inquisitive team, I had enjoyed my visit. As I learned more about their aim of making philanthropic giving more effective, I had been rather intrigued. But my hands and mind had since been full with leaving Tearfund and starting Integral.

Now Steve was asking me whether I'd consider joining him and helping lead efforts to try to revolutionize the world of philanthropy through Geneva Global.

PART TWO:

THE BIRTH OF PERFORMANCE PHILANTHROPY

AROUND THE TIME I FIRST BEGAN EXPLORING some of the ways charitable organizations might multiply and maximize their impact, two very successful businessmen had started asking similar questions.

New Zealand–born brothers Richard and Christopher Chandler had earned admiration in the international-business community for the way they had, over a twenty-year period, quietly turned less than five million dollars from the sale of their family business into global assets of more than five billion dollars.[1] Though they maintained low personal profiles, they were known for astute, strategic investments and uncompromising business ethics.

They brought a similar focus to their philanthropic activities. Having long been concerned about a wide range of social issues and challenges around the world, they wanted to direct some of their wealth toward making a difference by allocating their charitable capital as prudently as they invested their other money. After some time studying the philanthropic world, they concluded that they would have more impact by supporting specific, locally based community organizations that were working on the ground, rather than large, international nongovernmental organizations (INGOs).

The question was how to know which grassroots groups to support. Having turned to investment banks in their business dealings, the Chandler brothers assumed that an equivalent philanthropic advisory service must surely exist somewhere. But they were unable to find one. Seeking to learn from

---

1. "Secrets of Sovereign," *Institutional Investor Magazine*, accessed December 2, 2014, http://www.institutionalinvestor.com/article.aspx?articleID=1019610&p=6#.VCyHnPldW7Y.

the efforts of others, they turned for advice to billionaire businessman Sir John Templeton, whose own philanthropic efforts included his self-named foundation.

During a lunch meeting at his London club in 1999, Sir John told them he didn't know of a philanthropic investment bank of the kind they were looking for but thought that it was a great idea. He encouraged them to start something like what they were describing, generously introducing them to the then CEO of his foundation, Charles Harper, to help get them started. Indeed, the first office was established just outside of Philadelphia, in the same location as the headquarters of the Templeton Foundation.

So Geneva Global began there. Initially established to invest the Chandlers' own philanthropic monies as wisely as possible, over time the firm grew to offer similar services to others who learned of the organization and also wanted to take a more businesslike approach to their giving.

The Chandlers appointed Eric Thurman as Geneva Global's first CEO, and with his help, the organization adapted many of the lessons from the brothers' experience investing in the global finance industry to refine the proprietary, research-based, outcome-driven investment model that had served them so well in their emerging-market forays. In order to sift through a diverse range of philanthropic investment opportunities, they developed prospectuses that set out detailed risk assessments, personnel reviews, and outcome expectations to assist in deciding where, what, and whom to support.

While these research reports guided the decision-making process, they were also balanced by the production of post-investment reports that provided clear metrics on the outcomes achieved. This was no Pollyanna, do-good exercise; it was designed to understand on-the-ground challenges to get better results and to get them at scale.

In this way, Geneva Global facilitated a step change from traditional money-led charitable giving—the traditional role of a foundation essentially being a pot of money to be scattered among the poor—toward a sharpened focus on results and accountability.

From its very inception, the organization was focused on maximizing the returns available from each philanthropic dollar invested. This was not only the beginning of outcome-driven philanthropy designed to provide the maximum good for the greatest number, it was being done at an institutional scale, with Geneva Global handling millions of dollars annually. Over a thousand projects were funded in over a hundred countries.

Geneva Global was never intended to be the largest, but it has always aspired to be the best at directing scarce philanthropic capital toward where it can make the greatest enduring difference in the lives of the disadvantaged.

As the enterprise and its impact grew, Steve Beck, who was promoted to become Geneva Global's second CEO in 2006, realized that they needed someone who had run a bigger organization in the international-development world to promote the overseas research work and invited me to join the organization. Meanwhile, I had recognized that seeing the kind of large-scale results I dreamed of in international development required a different model than had been available up to that point. The two needs seemed like an ideal match, and so I joined the company.

In 2007, as the economic crisis was brewing, the decision was made that Geneva Global should become an independent business. This outcome was realized in September 2008, when I bought the organization the day after Lehman Brothers collapsed, wondering all the while about the wisdom of owning a philanthropic professional-services company as the economy was spiraling downward. Fortunately our experiences in servicing wealthy individuals, inherent investment thinking, and attention to detail in metrics, results, and lessons learned appealed to a changing philanthropic marketplace, and we survived.

Anyone who is part of a successful long-term relationship will tell you that initial attraction is followed by a period of adjustment as you learn and understand each other before coming to a place of mutual fulfillment.

That has been true of Geneva Global over the past decade as we have melded the best of our backgrounds, experiences, and insights. Seeing the Chandler brothers' vision become a reality has not been without its challenges; you don't innovate without having to learn and change as you go. We've revised and refined our principles and practices in light of experience and greater understanding.

Throughout it all, Christopher Chandler's support has continued uninterrupted, and he remains one of our largest clients to this day. Since 2006, Chandler's legacy of philanthropic innovation, which began with Geneva Global in 1999, has evolved into our partnership in the bold initiatives of the Legatum Foundation[2], which is run by the private investment firm Legatum.

The degree to which we have been successful can best be measured not only by the millions of lives changed annually through our work but also by the growing number of other organizations, agencies, individuals, and families who seek us out for help in doing good great.

THE EIGHT PILLARS OF PERFORMANCE PHILANTHROPY

Our approach is founded on eight essential pillars that we believe should form the basis of purposeful, effective philanthropy. They are a frame of reference for anyone looking to spend their money well in the cause of change. They define what we call performance philanthropy—a rigorous and results-oriented approach to creating positive social impact.

At its heart, this is about great service to those on both ends, the recipients and the donors. We help people in need more when we measure and evaluate what we are doing. Meaning well is not enough.

---

2. Legatum Foundation, accessed December 2, 2014, http://www.legatum.org.

Part of being more effective involves treating the donors better. Considering it is a service-based sector focused on doing good, much of the charitable world actually does a pretty poor job of serving the givers. At Geneva Global, we believe that, by better serving those who want to help make a difference in the world, we can ultimately achieve more because we ensure that they spend their money well and are, in turn, hopefully inspired to do more.

Our performance philanthropy principles, or pillars, have been refined through experience in bringing help and effecting change around the world, from remote villages to busy urban centers.

INVESTMENT THINKING

We need to be more businesslike in our approach to doing good, bringing head and heart together. Why be satisfied with less return for what you give to a charity than you would in giving the same amount to a broker?

METHODICAL MEASURING

If you don't count and evaluate what you are doing, you can never know how effective you are or how much more you could achieve. You need to ask hard questions of the people who want to use your money.

SUCCESSFUL FAILING

The world is only getting more complex, and we can't solve today's problems with yesterday's answers. That requires innovation and creativity, the willingness to try new things, and the ability to learn from mistakes and adapt.

LOCAL IMPLEMENTING

With a few exceptions, most effective development work is done by organizations that are rooted and established in the communities they are serving—more so than by even the most willing outsiders.

STRATEGIC PLANNING

A lot of development work is based on "silo" thinking: looking at situations in single-issue terms. But so many issues are complex, interwoven, and need to be approached from multiple angles to achieve a real tipping point for positive change.

DELIBERATE MULTIPLYING

Help for today is vital, but what can be done to ensure the same problem doesn't pop up again tomorrow or next door? We must look for ways to further leverage all that we are doing.

ACTIVE COLLABORATING

The combined total can be greater than the sum of the individual parts. By deliberately bringing implementers and donors together in partnership ventures, it is possible to set and achieve bigger goals.

FORWARD LOOKING

As much as we have developed some firm convictions about how to do good better, we recognize that it is important to remain open to change as cultural and technological shifts impact the world, its needs, and the possible solutions.

INVESTMENT THINKING

IMAGINE YOU WANT A NEW CAR and decide to visit the dealer whose big-smile ads you've seen on billboards and television. He greets you warmly, pumps your hand, asks if you'd like a cup of coffee, and then gets down to business.

"So you're looking for a new car?" he asks enthusiastically. "Well, you came to the right place! I can help."

It seems like you chose a good dealer with whom to do business.

"Now, let's not get bogged down by which model has the better repair record or gives you the best mileage," he says, rubbing his hands. "Instead, what's your favorite color?"

Absurd, of course. Much as you might prefer blue over red, you'd probably go elsewhere to find your next vehicle. But in many ways, that's how things go when people are looking to give money to charitable endeavors. There's not a lot of attention given to particulars and performance; the focus is more on the aesthetics.

The first, overarching point in effective philanthropy, we believe, is to be more businesslike about charity—to develop an investment mind-set: what exactly are you getting for what you give? You have to kick the tires, so to speak.

To be fair, I have met some benefactors who simply choose not to examine the details of what happens to the money they give away. They've made it by using their heads, they explain, so they want their hearts to determine where and how they share some of those rewards. It feels purer to them somehow.

And there is also something to be said for leaving the specifics of the job to those with more expertise in the charity world. While people in business do have much wisdom and insight to offer to the philanthropic community, not everything there is transferable. The world of effecting social change is much more complex than commerce.

So I understand the reluctance of some to ask too many questions when it comes to what they donate. But just as a savvy customer would want to look under the hood of the new sports car whose color he or she likes, I believe anyone looking to help make a difference in the world will have the greatest impact and be most fulfilled when bringing both heart and head into the endeavor.

Apart from anything else, by applying a more businesslike approach to donors' philanthropic efforts and improving the results of what they are involved in, they can increase the sense of satisfaction they derive. Feeling good about helping make the world better for others is perfectly natural. So feeling better about being able to do even more good only makes even more sense.

We just can't ignore this emotional factor. And it's not limited to the world of philanthropy. I was astonished to find how much gut feeling was involved in business during my time in the stock market. I arrived thinking that decisions were all based on the numbers and trends we dissected and analyzed, but I soon discovered how significant emotions were.

After due diligence, we'd present our best recommendations, but it would take only a slightly negative comment about a stock in the morning's issue of the *Financial Times* for our traders to get nervous and want to sell. Prices would fall, people would get scared and disinvest in a hurry, and the market would lurch.

The point is not to dismiss the emotional element involved in philanthropy but to balance it. Indeed, passion is a prerequisite for wanting to bring about change. We all need something to drive us on when things get challenging— and they do when you try to intervene in entrenched areas like injustice.

There's also a sense in which greater giving means raised responsibility. Someone donating twenty-five dollars a month to help feed and school an orphan may not feel the need to dig deep into financial statements to see how well that money is being spent. But if you were giving thousands to build an orphanage, it would make sense to want to be sure how the funds are being used. Or even if building another orphanage is a good idea in the first place.

Indeed, some philanthropists admit to feeling a sort of peer pressure to be seen to do good well. They have earned a reputation for handling money effectively in their business life, and they don't want to be considered irresponsible when it comes to their charitable efforts.

One downside of this understandable concern is that it can encourage people to gravitate toward "safer" funding, supporting only tried and trusted programs. This isn't necessarily a bad thing, but just as with financial investments, sometimes the greatest returns are in the riskiest efforts. There should be room for innovative approaches that may fail but could also yield enormous benefit. This penchant for following the giving of well-known names also ends up overfunding some causes and neglecting others just as worthy and sometimes ripe for creating significantly more impact.

THERE IS NO BETTER PLACE to see how developing an investment mind-set—an intentional approach to addressing a problem—can help bring about more substantive change than in the Valley of the Blind.

The name was given to Luapula Province in northeastern Zambia years ago, and based on the word "impofu," the Chibemba name for the blind.[1] The region has long been one of the poorest in a nation where nearly 75 percent of the population earns less than $1.25 per day.[2] A long-hidden factor

---

1. Geoffrey Salisbury, *Yesterday's Safari* (Sussex, England: The Book Guild Limited, 1990), 71.

2. "Zambia Statistics," UNICEF (2011), accessed December 2, 2014, http://www.unicef.org/infoby-country/zambia_statistics.html.

behind the area's grinding poverty is an unusually high level of blindness that gave it the grim nickname; some 4 percent of the million or so population has lost sight. As early as the 1950s, this valley was notable for its excessive blindness; a survey of the time recorded that one child in every thirty and one adult in every forty-five was blind.[3]

Blindness is a major life challenge wherever you may live but significantly more so in the developing world. There are no assistance programs, no disability aids, and no support services in Luapula. When you lose your sight in these regions, you essentially lose your life and your value. You not only become a burden to your family, you are something of a shame. Many blind people are left alone in a back room somewhere.

The blind in Luapula have white sticks, but not to help them navigate their way around on their own as in the West. Typically they are used for someone else to lead the unsighted person around. It's common to see young children walking ahead of an unsighted grandparent, holding onto their white stick like a long relay runner's baton. Caused by typically slow-onset infections and diseases, blindness now affects a much higher proportion of older adults, but young people and even children can lose their sight too.

Those affected suffer prejudice and loss of self-worth. When I visited the area, I met a woman whose husband had divorced her and married someone else because she could no longer see. But the effects go further and deeper than the individuals afflicted. The blind are unable to work and provide for their families and, thus, become a further burden in already struggling homes and communities.

Not only was blindness a major root of poverty in Luapula for many years, it was also something that could be addressed fairly simply. Many people lost their sight due to easily treated or correctable problems like trachoma and cataracts. Poor hygiene standards were a large part of the problem.

---

3. John Wilson, *Travelling Blind* (London: The Adventurers Club, 1964), 123.

It wasn't that there were no efforts being made to tackle the situation, though they were admittedly limited. The problem was that the attempts were not being made in a comprehensive and coordinated manner. What was needed was a plan that addressed all the issues, from prevention to treatment—an investment approach that sought a long-term return.

As we researched the situation on behalf of a client interested in helping make an enduring difference in the region, we found very limited medical care available. By way of example, the Roman Catholic sisters running St. Paul's Mission Hospital in a town called Kashikishi were well aware of and concerned about the high rate of blindness, but all they could offer was a monthly eye clinic by a visiting ophthalmologist based at another hospital several hours' drive away.

Lack of available medical treatment meant that many people turned to alternative methods of treatment, including traditional healers. Unfortunately, the healers' solution only added to the problems. They would grind stones into a paste that was applied to the affected eyes, not surprisingly causing further damage. When people would then eventually go to the hospital for help, their condition would be much worse and less likely to be treatable. That, in turn, reinforced the widely held view that the hospital was ineffective, keeping people from going there when earlier treatment might have helped.

It was a vicious cycle, and one that would only keep repeating if it weren't addressed. Handing out more medicine alone would not be enough. Breaking the cycle involved a creative response.

Rather than criticizing the locally respected village healers, for whom traditional methods were a source of income, we decided to co-opt them. Through discussions with representative leaders, we were able to recruit the healers as first responders, training them to identify common eye conditions, offer basic medications where appropriate, and make referrals for more comprehensive care where needed. The fees they earned replaced the income they lost as people abandoned the damaging traditional treatments. We also drew traditional birth assistants, teachers, and community health workers into the endeavor, training them to understand and identify eye conditions. This army of local volunteers became an important screening and referral network.

All this meant increased demand on clinic and hospital services, so it was important to improve the situation there as well. We trained health workers in clinics in basic eye care, simple cataract operations, and evaluations. We equipped a proper eye clinic and ward at St. Paul's Hospital so that more complicated surgeries could be performed there.

Then we had to do something about basic patient services like scheduling transportation and operations. It sounds obvious from a Western perspective, but it isn't so easy in parts of the world where limited resources and man power, along with poor infrastructure, mean the very few ambulances there arrive when they are supposed to.

Treatment was important, but so too was prevention. This involved finding organizations to run education programs to prevent trachoma. Going from village to village, they would use short plays to dramatize the importance of things like building community latrines. Providing designated places, rather than just making any clear space they could find a bathroom, helped isolate a major source of infection. Emphasizing the importance of washing your face and not sharing the same face cloths across the whole family, to avoid spreading germs, was also important.

In the seven years since this strategic, multifaceted initiative began, thousands of people have been treated in the early stages of eye disease, preventing their conditions from worsening. The number of people seeking medical treatment has gone up dramatically; cataract surgeries increased fourfold as a result of the program. The trachoma-prevention program will keep thousands from getting the disease.

One of the patients I met at St. Paul's while visiting the area was a mother of three who had never seen her children, having lost her sight when she herself was young. When hospital staff removed the pads from her eyes after the operation to restore her vision, she clapped her hands in delight and exclaimed, "I never realized my dress was so pretty!" She was tremendously thankful—and anxious to return home to look at her children for the first time.

Seeing this situation as an intentional investment that demands a good social return meant that, in Zambia, we created a systemic, multifaceted set of coordinated interventions. To the people of Luapula, it means the Valley of the Blind's sad label will soon no longer be appropriate.

ALTHOUGH WE BELIEVE philanthropy should be viewed as an investment market like any other (looking for the greatest possible return), it's also important to recognize that it is one that is much more inherently inefficient and unstable—dysfunctional even. Costs often are not known, it's hard to get common benchmarks to use for comparisons, and performance measures are many times not comparable between different organizations involved.

And though this may sound surprising, it's actually every bit as competitive a market as the rest. Organizations are competing for donors in the same ways businesses compete for customers. Indeed, that's the point: donors are customers. This means that organizations espousing the same cause need to set themselves apart from the rest. One way they do that is by the stories they tell. Some groups are supremely effective at the way they communicate the need, but the stories don't always stand up to close scrutiny.

Greg Mortenson's charity, celebrated for building schools in Pakistan and Afghanistan, was adversely affected after his 2007 bestseller, *Three Cups of Tea: One Man's Mission to Promote Peace...One School at a Time*, was discredited.

Somaly Mam, named one of *TIME* magazine's 100 Most Influential People of 2009 for her anti-sex-trafficking work in Cambodia, resigned in 2014 from the foundation that she had established after some of her accounts were proven to be false.

Sometimes it's not what organizations say that matters; it's what they don't tell you that matters. Some groups with impressive websites that spotlight a particular need don't make it clear that they outsource all the actual work to other, existing organizations without adding any value of their own to the process. They are really middlemen, taking the opportunity to raise money by marketing a need.

Some groups have an almost elitist attitude, as though they are doing you a favor in taking your money, so they certainly don't need to give a detailed account for it. Most organizations do recognize the need to offer some level of accountability for what they do with the money they are given, but these efforts are often more opaque than truly transparent—and typically as minimalist as possible to major donors.

It is also important to recognize that weighing one agency's program against another's is not necessarily comparing apples to apples. This group may say it can provide a cow for a poor family in Asia for five hundred dollars, while another does so for two thousand dollars. What you cannot know without digging deep and doing some analysis is that the first simply hands over the animal with a few quick tips on how to take care of it, while the second does so only after the beneficiary family completes some animal-husbandry training that ensures the long-term health of the creature.

Which is the more effective charity at the end of the day?

Clearly, I believe it is the one that makes a longer-lasting impact, thereby offering a greater return on investment. This—a level of sustainability—is a vital factor if we are to affect true, lasting change. Sadly, too many philanthropic efforts in the past have only encouraged dependency in one way or another, actually undermining the very sense of dignity they were seeking to foster in those being served.

This is part of a challenge unique to the philanthropic market: the danger of unintended consequences when someone sets out to solve one problem but inadvertently causes another one, maybe even worse.

I saw this firsthand in northern Mozambique when I was visiting to learn about what was being done to tackle the country's AIDS crisis. While driving through Chimoio, I noticed a large factory building that seemed to be idle, though it was in good shape. I asked my hosts about the place.

They told me it had been a clothing factory that had supplied much of the region and employed many people.

"So what happened?"

One of my companions pointed west, to the border with Zimbabwe, about thirty miles away.

"Westerners were sending free used clothes to Zimbabwe to help the people there," he said. "Some Zimbabweans started coming across the border into Mozambique with the clothes. They'd sell them for less than it cost to make them locally, and eventually the factory in Chimoio went out of business.

"Everyone lost their jobs."

Of course the Europeans and Americans donating their cast-off clothes to help the needy in one part of Africa had no idea they were causing hardship for others elsewhere.

The same was true for those funding antislavery efforts in Sudan, which became the subject of considerable suspicion.

With widespread reports of people being abducted and sold into slavery during the height of the civil war in the early 2000s, some organizations decided to intervene by buying back the freedom of those who had been taken. But when my Tearfund team began exploring the locations where the slave rescues had reportedly been taking place, we could find no trace of anyone who had been bought back. They all seemed to have disappeared.

From the inquiries we were able to make, it seemed that, most likely, what was happening was a fraud ring. People would be captured, bought back, and then captured again, with everyone getting a cut along the way.

I tell these stories not to deter anyone from giving money but to underscore the importance of due diligence. They also spotlight how important it can be to have people who understand the language, the culture, and the context in the area, on the ground, to help ensure that good intentions get translated into good practice.

Being in any way critical of relief and development programs is frowned upon a bit by some because it seems churlish; after all, these people are all trying to help, right? That may be true, but good intentions are not enough. We all know how the road to hell is paved, and all I can think of is how much money has been wasted on the asphalt that could have been spent elsewhere.

Ill-informed philanthropy needs to be addressed not only because it wastes money and resources directly but also because it undermines the good being done by others. When people get burned by groups that turn out to be less than they claimed to be in one way or another, donors can become suspicious and cynical, perhaps even becoming discouraged from giving to others who are doing good work well.

One of the challenges of applying an investment approach to philanthropy is that there is no common or agreed currency, so to speak. People set their own values, and who is to say what is right and what is wrong?

When I was leading Tearfund in England, some of those I knew who were involved in international relief and development used to both chuckle and admit to a feeling of exasperation at the success of a particular domestic charity that ran a home for retired donkeys. It seemed to have no shortage of funds for what it needed to do, while many of my peers were often desperately trying to find funding to keep important programs helping humans going. But the fact is that some people are concerned about the plight of animals, and who is to tell them that they should not be?

Then there is the question of returns. In the financial world, this is fairly easy to gauge. You put x amount into something, and you expect y to come back. Dollars in, dollars out. A specific amount of seed, and an expected yield. But in the world of philanthropy, it is not always so clear an equation.

For the most part, philanthropy has historically been measured by just the *in* part. How much did someone give to a particular cause or concern? But that's no gauge of what was actually achieved as a result.

Economist and coauthor of the best-selling book, *Freakanomics: A Rogue Economist Explores the Hidden Side of Everything*, Steven D. Levitt put it well in a *Wall Street Journal* article when he said, "With philanthropists, much of the benefit and the accolades come when you give the money, not when you solve the problem, which I think is kind of backward.

"Nobody [is] really asking if their money does any good in the world."

When we talk at Geneva Global about doing great, not just good, we're getting into the area of social change, which is extremely difficult to measure. It's not just about how many meals may be given to hungry children, for example. What does that mean in terms of their ability and willingness to go to school? And how does improved education benefit the greater community? How might feeding someone lunch today impact the community in a few years' time? The effects may spread out far, like ripples from a stone dropped into a pool.

From our years of experience, we have developed a seven-point process that helps us assess new opportunities and local organizations to fund on behalf of our clients. Just as private equity managers evaluate factors, such as the strength of the management team involved, as part of their due diligence, we conduct a thoroughgoing assessment of possible organizations.

We ask questions about everything from governance to bookkeeping to reputation to relationships with others. When evaluating a potential new initiative, we want to know the following:

CONTEXT: What is the bigger picture? What factors outside the control of the organization concerned could keep it from meeting the goals? How might those risks be reduced?

CLARITY: Does the organization show that it understands the complexities of the situation? Does its program reflect the needs, and is the projected impact reasonable?

COHERENCE: What is the organization's experience and track record in the region? Is it up to the challenge of the program, and does the project integrate well with other initiatives in the same area?

CAPABILITY AND CAPACITY: Do the leaders of the organization have the experience needed? Does the organization have a stable history? How well staffed is it, and how well trained and resourced are they?

CREDIBILITY: What kind of reputation does the group have? How financially transparent is it? Are there any connections to other organizations that might be of concern?

CONTINUOUS IMPROVEMENT: How does the organization intend to monitor its effectiveness during the program and make changes or improvements as necessary? What kind of internal development systems are there?

As you might expect, this is not a quick process, but it offers a frame of reference that measures more than an organization's ability to touch potential donors' hearts with slick marketing.

They are the sort of questions that come with an investment-philanthropy mind-set. Some donors will want to grapple with them for themselves, perhaps taking advantage of some of the groups that attempt to rank organizations according to their effectiveness. For others, Geneva Global was founded. We ask and help find answers for the hard questions that need to be addressed to ensure effective philanthropy.

METHODICAL MEASURING

IF YOU SPEND ANY AMOUNT OF TIME WITH ME, you might notice that every now and then, I will steal a glance at my right wrist. It's not that I'm bored and checking my watch to see what time it is. Those peeks are at a silicon bracelet that is helping to keep me healthy.

Having tried to stay in relatively good shape most of my life, it was sobering to have my doctor express some concerns about my health during a recent checkup. I'd be fine, he assured me, as long as I took—literal—steps to keep on top of things. That meant being a bit more careful about my diet and making sure I get more exercise every day.

I run as my schedule permits, but that's not always possible with so much travel, so I have begun to walk whenever and wherever I can—for instance, using my own two feet to get between meetings when I am in New York City or Washington, DC, rather than traveling by subway. I also take the stairs rather than an elevator. I'm supposed to take so many steps a day, which I track on my fitness bracelet. It can also record my weight and monitor my sleep patterns.

All that is ensuring I actually do something about maintaining my health. But without some specific goals, like distance and calories and a way of keeping tabs on my progress, chances are my doctor's warning and my own good intentions would not be enough to motivate me. I need instant and accurate feedback to keep me focused and on track.

A long and healthy life is important enough for me to want to do what I can to realize that potential, and the same principle applies when it comes to other people's lives. I want a way to encourage maximum positive impact in theirs.

Measurement and metrics are an integral part of business life, of course. No company would get far without sales goals, progress reports, projections, and spreadsheets. The old business maxim still rings true: if you can't measure it, you can't manage it.

Yet that guiding principle largely seems to be ignored when it comes to philanthropy. It's not that there's a complete absence of numbers and statistics, but for the most part, what you have is counting, not measuring.

An organization will, perhaps, report how many children were enrolled on the first day of school or tally the number of people who were fed in a given year, but there's no assessment of what was actually really achieved as a result. For instance, the children could all have dropped out of school, never returning after the first day. The figures describe intent, rather than defining impact. They are about activity, not results.

Such numbers can seem impressive while being quietly evasive. For example, some donor-supported religious radio broadcasters talk about serving a listening audience of so many millions. That might be the number of people who live in the area their transmitters reach, but how many actually have access to a radio? And how many understand the language the programs are broadcast in? And how many really tune in when the shows are on?

Why the all-too-common reluctance to measure philanthropic efforts? For one thing, it's hard to do. Another factor is the fear of failure. Raising money is highly competitive, so organizations vying with each other for donor funds usually want to be seen as responsibly handling the money they are given.

This nervousness about being scrutinized too closely is all the more unfortunate when you consider that a certain amount of failure is an accepted fact in the business world. If you aren't having to reevaluate, recalibrate, and reassess, you are probably not being innovative enough to bring anything new to the market. Progress involves the occasional steps backward. Businessmen and women understand that. As long as your overall momentum is forward, missteps are OK.

The closest a lot of charitable organizations come to offering any level of financial self-assessment is in reporting how much of their income goes to overhead. This benchmark is commonly included in charities' annual reports, revealing the amount of income spent on things other than the actual programs themselves, such as fund-raising and administrative overhead. Combined, these two elements are typically held under 25 percent, otherwise donors often start to raise eyebrows.[1] That leaves 75 percent of funding for program costs.

But while the majority of money ostensibly goes to program costs, the reality is that it all gets a little fuzzy. There is no guarantee that the other 75 percent all finds its way directly to the vaccination clinics or drilling of wells for which it is being given. Sometimes expenditure that should more appropriately fall under overhead gets accounted for in program expenses, such as travel for anyone associated with the initiative. A percentage of the salaries of anyone who has anything even remotely to do with the project—maybe preparing or editing a report—could be included. Not that some of these other program costs are wrong or even wasteful. Donor education, advocacy in Western countries, national offices in the field, and headquarter relations with government are certainly useful and needed. For donors wishing to primarily support the organization, they may be wise investments. However, if your focus is about getting the maximum portion of your donation to a local project, then you might want to dig deeper to understand just how much money reaches the end beneficiary.

And then there's the fact that, without some independent benchmarks, even knowing the percentage of fund-raising and administrative costs isn't enough information on which to make an informed giving decision. Too many times you can end up comparing apples and oranges. Indeed, the only real apples-to-apples comparison I know of is that of comparing the percentage of a donation that goes to the local project on the ground—whether managed by an INGO or a locally based organization. Based on what leaders at INGOs have candidly disclosed to me over the years, I know that this percentage is typically 50 to 66 percent of the donation. However, very

---

1. A. Gregory and D. Howard, "The Nonprofit Starvation Cycle," *Stanford Social Innovation Review*, fall 2009, accessed December 2, 2014, http://www.ssireview.org/articles/entry/the_nonprofit_starvation_cycle/.

few charities publish or disclose this level of information. Unfortunately, that means you will have to be very persistent in hunting down the data you need to understand how your donation is being allocated.

If one organization's administration and fund-raising costs are 30 percent, but you know that it has systems and procedures in place that ensure a higher return on investment for the remaining 70 percent, doesn't it make more sense to donate there rather than to a group reporting a 20 percent combined overhead but with a much lesser return? Overhead alone is simply not a good measure of effective granting.

Challenging this long-standing way of looking at how charities use money has ruffled some feathers. It requires a level of transparency and openness on the part of the recipient organization that many are uncomfortable with. They prefer to be accepted as the experts and left to get on with their work, offering progress reports that may include some heartwarming stories but not much substance.

Ironically, my experience has been that donors are more confident when they find themselves dealing with organizations that are more open in their reporting. Trust seems to go up when they are told, "Actually, this project didn't quite turn out the way we had hoped, and here are the reasons why."

That's because—and it's important to remember—much philanthropic activity occurs in challenging environments. We're not talking about sterile, safe laboratories where external factors can be controlled and eliminated. Programs are conducted in parts of the world where there is environmental, climatic, political, financial, and social instability. There are any number of reasons a project may fail that could have nothing to do with its design or implementation—factors way beyond the control of any organization.

However, having systems in place that require some assessment of what happened can be beneficial in identifying situations and circumstances that may not be possible to avoid in the future but that can be planned or prepared for to some degree. In this way, a failure can actually help increase the likelihood of more future successes so that even the initial money isn't wasted ultimately. As Thomas Edison famously said, "I haven't failed. I've just found ten thousand ways that won't work."

METRICS AND MEASUREMENT HAVE BEEN AN INTEGRAL PART of an effort Geneva Global has undertaken to tackle Ethiopia's education crisis, which, like an unseen riptide, keeps sucking the country under.

People in the West readily think of famine when Ethiopia is mentioned, but it's not just an absence of food. Poverty and poor health are inextricably linked to low levels of learning in the east African nation, which an international report has named as one of the six worst places in the world, education-wise, to be a child, and where nearly two out of three people are illiterate. Around a third of school-age children in the country do not complete primary school.[2]

There are serious ripple effects of missing out on education, especially for young girls. They are more likely to marry young, have children at an early age, and contract and die from preventable diseases.

By carefully tracking an effort to reverse the high dropout rate over the past few years, we have been able to develop a program that not only offers real hope for Ethiopia but could serve as a model for dealing with education problems in other countries.

I first came across the Speed School idea on the other side of the continent. A Norwegian organization called Strømme Foundation was funding programs in Mali that targeted some of the many children who were of school age but not attending classes—many because their impoverished parents needed help earning money and looking after younger siblings. Through a nine-month accelerated learning course, a Speed School,

2. *Back to School? The Worst Places in the World to be a School Child in 2010*, Global Campaign for Education, 2010, accessed December 2, 2014, http://www.campaignforeducation.org/docs/reports/1goal/1Goal%20School%20Report.pdf.

children were brought up to the skill level that would enable them to pass public-school entrance exams and rejoin—or, for some, join for the first time—the government school system.

Bringing together two private foundations in a joint project, the Strømme Foundation and the Legatum Foundation, we launched the three-year West Africa Children's Strategic Initiative, which took Speed Schools to other communities not only across Mali but also Niger and Burkina Faso. More than thirty-four thousand children were enrolled in Speed Schools, with almost twenty-six thousand of them passing final exams and going on to government schools.

Encouraged by these measurable results, the Legatum Foundation asked us to develop a similar initiative in Ethiopia. With the information we gathered from west Africa, we were able to fine-tune the program for Ethiopia, which included adding an extra month of schooling.

Local leaders have to request Speed Schools for their communities, ensuring essential community buy-in. They also need to provide the building that will be used for the ten months that the speed learning is offered there. It might be a vacant house, an unused government school building, or a church like the one I visited on the shores of Lake Awasa in the Great Rift Valley. The project then equips the classrooms with furniture and materials.

Having learned that oversized classes in government schools contribute to the high dropout rate, the Speed Schools are limited to twenty-five children per class. There, high-school and college graduates who have undergone training teach the students. Following a standardized curriculum, they guide their students through basic numeracy and literacy in three languages: their tribal tongue, the national Amharic language, and English. Upon completing the ten-month program in one area, the Speed School moves on and offers classes in another community.

To date, around fifty thousand Ethiopian children have gone through Speed School classes, with around 98 percent of them passing the government entrance exams. It's true that these tests are not very demanding, but the potential from having so many more children back in school is huge.

A critical component we have included in Speed Schools in Ethiopia, as a result of evaluating how things went in west Africa, has been self-help groups for parents, primarily the mothers. We learned that they needed some incentives for encouraging their children to pursue education, as they would be losing the help they had been getting around the home and on the land.

Even when they were keen for the youngsters to learn, there was often a big financial barrier to parents sending the kids to classes. While government schools are free, families have to cover the cost of uniforms and books—a significant investment in a hugely impoverished country.

Through the self-help groups, women have been encouraged to start small businesses and create income-generating activities that enable their children to go to school. By bringing mothers together for mutual support, we found they developed savings plans to pay for school supplies and also got some basic literacy training themselves, which in turn spurred their desire to see their children learn more.

We continue to refine the program as we learn more. An ad hoc follow-up survey by education researchers from England who have been studying the Speed School initiative found that a year after completing the course, only about two-thirds of the students were still continuing their education in the government schools. Though the survey wasn't detailed enough to help us understand exactly what was happening, we were disappointed and concerned. It was a red flag.

We realized that while the Speed School itself may be successful in preparing children for regular school, we needed to find ways to improve the likelihood of their continuing their education. So we have been looking at ways of addressing the issue as part of the Speed School program, involving the parent groups, and, perhaps, instituting some sort of buddy system for children going into government schools to encourage them to keep attending.

One of the frustrations of the project we undertook in west Africa was that we were unable to gather all the data we would have liked to help us better gauge the effectiveness of the program. In Ethiopia, however, we hope to be able to track the outcome over the next ten years, looking not just at enrollment rates back into government schools but how an increase in education impacts poverty and health markers.

Cause and effect certainly isn't always easy to quantify. And issues relating to relief and development are hugely interwoven and complex—it's three-dimensional chess again. But even attempting to understand the data is important if organizations are to develop and improve so that they can do more tomorrow because of what they have learned today.

THE KIND OF ANALYSIS AND METRICS that are helping us fine-tune the Speed School concept demand somewhat of a different approach to donor programs. They require much more than wanting to do good; they demand having some clear, identifiable, and measurable goals ahead of philanthropic action.

For many local organizations, this is a stretch. They aren't used to being so detailed or providing donors—other than governments or big foundations—so much information, and they don't have the systems in place or the trained staff to do the sort of accounting we require. Some self-select out of our funding at this point because they don't want to jump through what they see as unnecessary or unattainable hoops. For others who seek the benefits of our approach, we are able to offer training and support that may enable them to fulfill our reporting requirements.

While recording results is important, we're not looking to tie organizations up in meaningless paperwork. I remember how time-consuming and taxing it can be to fulfill reporting requirements from my time in Liberia. It can all seem a bit unnecessary when you're out there trying to actually help people. And if you are receiving grants from multiple donors, it can mean providing different kinds of reports for each group. Well aware of this potential danger, we advocate collaborative reporting requirements that can meet each donor's requirements for the least time invested.

Nevertheless, the assessment process does take time and effort. Creating a baseline against which to measure results, a grid of goals, expectations, and success markers is hard work, but it helps sharpen the focus of the endeavor and then provide realistic benchmarks for improvement or adaptation.

Drilling down into numbers and statistics in this way also helps donors clarify and identify in what and where they want to try to help make a difference. Some may simply want to impact as many people as they can for as little cost as possible per person. The program targeting neglected tropical diseases (or NTDs, as they are known) that we ran for the Legatum Foundation in Burundi and Rwanda is an example of a program that benefitted a lot of people, but in a relatively shallow manner.

For less than thirty cents per person per year, more than eight million people were treated for four largely overlooked diseases that, combined, have a crippling effect in Africa. Spread by insects and worms, diseases like trachoma and schistosomiasis have a disastrous impact. They cause blindness and malnutrition, which, in turn, lead to developmental problems and school absence that further perpetuates poverty. Those affected by these diseases often also face social stigma, especially when the diseases leave them disfigured. Low self-esteem leads to further loss of productivity.

With tracking systems in place, we were able to measure the results of this huge, three-year effort that included treatment and prevention education. Rates of schistosomiasis, a devastating disease caused by parasitic worms, were slashed by 85 percent in twelve pilot-study sites in Burundi, where it had been endemic, while in Rwanda, rates were reduced by 80 percent. Reinfection remains a serious issue, but the initiative has made significant inroads into a major problem for both countries for an annual cost of less than a can of soda per person.

At the other end of the scale are programs that require residential care and services, such as orphan care and schools for disabled children, or recovery and rehabilitation centers for those rescued from sex trafficking. Because of their facility- and labor-intensive nature, providing such programs can cost, per beneficiary, a hundred times what was needed to tackle the NTDs in Rwanda and Burundi.

Who is to say which is more worthwhile?

However, having these kinds of expense and result details enables donors to make informed decisions about where and how they want their money to make a difference. Some may be motivated to touch as wide a group of people as possible, while others may choose to focus on making a deeper impact in a more concentrated population.

Our investment approach starts by helping donors identify the level of risk they are comfortable with and the kind of return they would like to see. Determining how and where those two criteria intersect requires a careful evaluation of the different options available. And once a choice has been made, investment thinking means we will go back to see if that area is performing as expected, and if not, consider whether that money needs to be redeployed elsewhere. It is just irresponsible to keep putting money into a program that isn't achieving when the funds could make a difference elsewhere.

To assist clients in making informed giving decisions, Geneva Global has developed a series of detailed evaluations for organizations and programs. With the help of economists, analysts, and statisticians, we have created stringent guidelines for vetting projects. Since 2001, we have used them to evaluate 1,600 organizations in more than one hundred countries.

First, we look at outcomes rather than just outputs. In the case of water wells, for instance, we don't want to know simply how many wells may have been bored in a certain area; we are interested in finding out how incidence of waterborne diseases change as a result. That means having a longer-term view of projects. They aren't necessarily successful just because they have been completed.

A harsh reality is that, not long after they are drilled, a significant percentage of wells aren't providing clean water. They break down, and the parts aren't available for them to be repaired. Or the person trained in maintenance moves away. If such practical considerations aren't part of the planning, the program will fall short over time.

Because we believe it's important to set out specific goals and targets ahead of time, we're able to grade programs at the end. Those that significantly exceed expectations are rated as "overachieved." Any that are within 20 percent of projections get classified as "achieved." Those that meet less than 80 percent of the benchmarks that were set are considered to have "underachieved," while those that meet less than half the goals have "failed."

Another important part of our reporting is the cost-per-life-impact calculation. This attempts to work out how many lives have been impacted by the particular project and for how much per person. The figure can be weighed against costs for similar programs run by other groups to see how it measures up.

Finally, we have developed a sophisticated, proprietary social-impact index that looks at how much wider societal impact, beyond the immediate beneficiaries, a community development project may have. For example, in Ethiopia, what might be some of the long-term effects of getting children back into school? How could improved school attendance lead to better health, prosperity, and stability? We hope to find that out in the years to come.

Among the issues we consider in trying to evaluate the social-impact index are the degree to which a project impacts individual well-being and empowerment and in what ways social and cultural values that may contribute to existing conditions have been challenged or changed. We also ask, how well is this initiative supported by leaders of influence in the local community, the power brokers? How easily and well could this program be replicated?

These are not easy questions. Some are more qualitative than quantitative, and there's the natural tendency for organizations in the field to self-evaluate on a curve when asked for feedback. That has to be factored into the equation. We are now looking into ways of surveying actual beneficiaries, asking them directly how they feel about the services given to them, to get a more independent evaluation. Even this isn't foolproof, of course. In some cultures, people are prone to telling you what they think you want to hear.

Though assessments of this kind have their limits, we believe that it is imperative to give attention to developing a matrix of checks and questions that helps us judge fairly well just how much good has been done—and whether we may even be doing great.

SUCCESSFUL FAILING

EVERY YEAR WE PULL THE GENEVA GLOBAL TEAM TOGETHER at our Pennsylvania headquarters for a gathering we call Lessons Learned. Bringing in key field leaders from around the world and taking two weeks to focus on internal meetings makes the event a major investment in time and money. But we believe it's crucial to real success.

Typically, in my experience, many businesses and organizations prefer busyness to introspection and action to thought. But there can be great benefits from reversing the old maxim so that it becomes "don't just do something, sit there!"

For us, Lessons Learned is a time of important team building, training, and most of all, lots of deliberate reflection. We look back on what has worked and what hasn't. Having real data (projections and results) to examine is vital for meaningful assessment. We ask tough questions of each other and ourselves. The conversations are candid and not always comfortable, but everyone knows our time together is about being inquisitive, not holding an inquisition. There's also a good amount of laughter along the way.

When we initiated this practice, there were less than a dozen of us sitting informally around a conference table. Now that there are more than forty people involved, we have to be a little more structured, but we still try to maintain a certain informality.

Lessons Learned is not a witch hunt; it's a what hunt. What went right, and why? And what went wrong, and where? And what can we learn from all that for the future?

There has been an added bonus to this practice. As well as providing insights for improving programs, we have found that the time together reflecting like this has become an important way of reinforcing our organizational DNA, embedding our values. It's a glue that holds us together.

We don't keep our findings to ourselves either. As I have mentioned, we offer lessons-learned analyses in our reports to donors that address issues that have come up.

For example, our effort to eliminate trachoma in Zambia, where preventable blindness is a big concern, was set back seriously when the government told us that it couldn't provide all the medicine it had promised a week before the mass drug treatment program was to take place. Our program manager had to find a truck, drive to the capital city, and extract the drugs from the government warehouse to keep the program on track. Meanwhile, in China, implementation of programs aimed at helping children with special needs were set back months by red tape that held up the transfer of funds. Both situations were clearly beyond our control, but they did have a short-term negative impact on what we were doing.

Looking at how things have gone isn't just useful for the future, it helps us in the present. By watching progress closely, we are able to intervene when unforeseen problems arise and make adjustments or changes in a program before things get too far off track.

This kind of close attention is also helpful on the rare occasion we find that an organization one of our clients is funding turns out to not be quite as reliable, for one reason or another, as we had initially believed. When they learn that future funding is dependent on them fulfilling their current responsibilities, they are usually quick to address any issues or concerns.

But to be able to keep an eye on progress like this means you have to have local eyes looking out for the donor—someone on the ground caring about their interests.

Sometimes, despite all our best efforts and due diligence, things just don't go the way we had hoped or planned, and it isn't just a minor delay or setback like in Zambia and China. I'm talking about times when it's evident that the goals are simply not going to be reached to any significant measure.

When it becomes clear that what's needed is some major revision of the program or even reallocation of the funds, not just a little tweaking, we go back to the client with what we call a grant-modification request proposal. It explains why things haven't worked out and what we think should be done now and invites them to sign off on the changes.

We feel it's important for those who helped fund the original project to be informed and involved in the process, rather than quietly ignored and told later that things changed and the money went elsewhere—as can happen with some organizations. That doesn't develop trust or build a long-term relationship.

One time we helped a donor put money into a campaign to empower women's groups in Haiti. It was intended to help women start small businesses that would create more jobs and so improve health and education opportunities for children. We were impressed by the potential and the early progress reports. But as time went by, we became a little concerned.

There was a lot of noise, consultancy reports, workshops, and talk about what was going to be done. Yet as time went by, nothing actually seemed to be happening as a result. It was a lot of style but no substance. Eventually we decided it was best to cut our losses and recommend the supporter stop funding the program.

We thought we had done our due diligence beforehand, but when we went back and retraced our steps, we discovered where we had gone wrong. Part of our decision to go ahead in the first place had been based on the fact that the group concerned already had some funding from a major international organization. If this organization thought the proposal merited support, we'd reasoned, then it must be good.

This was an important reminder that it's easy to tolerate certain standards or levels of performance that might be widely accepted in the international-development community at large but really are not as exacting as they need to be. Though the particular program was not a success, we considered it a case of successful failing, in that we learned things that would help us better evaluate future projects.

Telling donors that the project they supported didn't work out is unusual, but we have found that it typically increases confidence. Our lessons-learned analyses detail the main factors for any failures or challenges faced. Some years ago, we examined previous projects that had underperformed. After reviewing and creating categories based on what had gone astray, we came to realize that there are typically three reasons why projects underperform. First, there are external factors beyond our control that can affect the situation on the ground, like natural disasters. Second, a lack of organization leadership and/or poor board governance can derail projects. Lastly, faulty assumptions can lead to poor project design, which often generates subpar performance.

We also take time during our annual Lessons Learned gathering to talk about what we have seen and heard about in other organizations. Are there ideas and practices that we need to consider and embrace? We know that we don't have all the answers ourselves, so we're keen to learn from others working in the same space.

All this requires an open kind of culture that encourages and rewards reflection and honesty. It's an attitude of humility and an openness to learning that I believe all international-development practitioners should employ. The Chandler brothers founded Geneva Global with the goal of finding ways that philanthropy could be done better—a vision, curiosity, and conviction I share and to which I have been able to bring not only some answers from my background and experience but also some additional questions of my own.

Maybe I was fortunate in who I worked with and for, or perhaps, it's just part of my makeup, but I have always felt that it's OK to make mistakes as long as you are trying your hardest and willing to learn and improve. I am grateful for one of my former business bosses, who told me once: "I don't mind if you make a mistake, just don't make it twice!"

Sadly, in my experience, many organizations in the philanthropic and business worlds don't value this sort of approach. There's a huge aversion to being seen as having made a mistake—better safe than sorry that it didn't work as you had hoped. It may be the reason why some donors gloss over or deny mistakes that may have been made or play it safe and grant to the same organizations as their peers, knowing they can deflect blame if things don't go according to plan. This kind of timidity can also be seen in the "paralysis of analysis," when overthinking a decision prevents any action from being taken.

Being open to critical evaluation requires a certain amount of humility. Maybe some charitable organizations fall short in this area because they fear that admitting they don't have all the answers and don't always get things right may make them look bad to potential donors. After all, someone who has money to give to a good cause wants to know it will be used well.

Sometimes you will hear charity leaders tell of mistakes, but these tend to be failures from the past, on other people's watch—the implication being that everything is OK now that they are in charge.

But, seriously, does anyone really believe that things go right 100 percent of the time? We all know that simply isn't reality. The kind of successful failing we look for is only possible when you are prepared to be honest and ask hard questions.

When an organization doesn't want to answer straight questions about their projects and finances and their failures as well as their successes, it is always a big red flag for me. It may not mean that they have anything to hide, but it does suggest a certain lack of confidence in who they are and what they do.

Another reason organizations can be reluctant to admit any weaknesses is that it implies others may have greater strengths in this area and potentially redirects a prospective donor elsewhere. That is a challenging consequence when you're competing for donor dollars.

For my part, I have always believed in being as honest as possible as a matter of principle, first and foremost. But it's also a matter of practicality; if I am straight with you, I don't have to try to remember how I may have spun something the last time we talked. And I have also found that directness is actually a successful strategy.

When I was back at Lucas Engineering & Systems for the second time, there was a lot of nervousness about what would happen to our consultancy unit as a result of the major changes that were taking place. There was much politicking and private chatter. People were fishing for information and jockeying for position. I felt myself getting sucked into it all but quickly became upset and disturbed. I realized that I just wasn't very good at all the backroom bargaining, and it stressed me out too much. So I excused myself from it all.

Not only did this relieve me of a lot of pressure, when the time came for people to speak up for others, pretty much everyone had good things to say about me because they said I was trustworthy. It was a big lesson for me.

Fear of failure also discourages innovation and risk, which are important elements in business and philanthropy alike. Just as commercial market forces change, rising and falling, so is the world of need in flux. Just because something worked twenty years ago does not mean it is necessarily the best way to respond to a need today, given the many changes that may have occurred over two decades. So we may need to try something new.

Innovation isn't always welcome, however, as I found out in Liberia. Our team was making desperately needed medicines available in Sinoe County once more, but I was concerned that the funding for the program would dry up within a year or so, and so would the supply of drugs. Everything would be back to square one. Why not charge people a nominal fee for the medications, rather than just give them away for free, I wondered. That way there would be more money to buy more drugs.

It would never work, I was told by others in the emergency-relief community. The area was just recovering from a devastating war. The people had no money, they said, and besides, they just needed help. Every other aid organization was giving away free drugs. But we were not doing them any favors by giving health care that would halt again in only a year once the emergency grant money ran out, I reasoned. Additionally, most people could find some way of paying for what really mattered to them, and doing so turned them from dependents to customers.

So we developed a three-tier, modest price list for the drugs we were providing. People did, indeed, find the nominal amount of money they needed to pay for them, and as a result, we were able to ensure that the supply continued for years—long after our team departed.

Now, with Geneva Global, I remain on the lookout for new ideas and approaches, even from other disciplines and sectors. I am always wondering if what works in one context may be taken, tweaked, and applied in another.

I first realized the importance of this when I was working as a consultant with Lucas and wrestling with some major internal-systems reorganization. I remembered what I had learned from a leading chain store while tracking the retail sector as a stockbroker. I had been impressed by its progressive supply chain systems, and while it handled food and clothes, I saw how some of the same concepts could be transferred to the world of auto parts and manufacturing.

One of our Geneva Global initiatives, a multifaceted program in Namibia, applies some of the change-management processes I learned at Lucas to integrating health services. Many principles of an effective supply chain are the same whether you are dealing with car parts or people and medicines. While at Lucas, I discovered how important it was to invite those who would be responsible for implementing any changes to be active stakeholders in the process. The same has proved true in Namibia, as all those with an active part in improving health—from hospitals to schools—have been recognized as stakeholders in the endeavor.

THERE'S NO CLEARER PICTURE of the need for openness to change when something is not working and flexibility in trying to meet changing world needs than you will find in Africa.

I will never forget being in Uganda in the early 2000s. As we drove out of the capital, it was as though Kampala was holding one huge funeral. The streets were lined with coffin makers piling up their rough wooden boxes one after the other for the latest AIDS victims. It was like an avenue of the dead. Not surprisingly, the disease was decimating the country. In one street I visited with members of the Tearfund project we were supporting, every third home had someone dying from the virus.

Much of the care consisted of nursing the sufferers as they faded and trying to help the orphaned children. The stress level on the caregivers was unbelievably high. African culture expects you to go to the funeral of someone you know, which meant that some of the volunteers were attending several funerals a week.

"I'm not sure how long we can keep doing this," one burned-out volunteer caregiver told me.

Within a few years, the challenge began to change. It wasn't that the crisis was over, it had simply morphed. Antiretroviral drugs became available in parts of the continent. For the first time, AIDS was no longer simply a death sentence. Those infected with the virus could expect to live longer, encouraging people to get tested and seek treatment.

Now there was a different issue. Large numbers of people with AIDS would be living longer. With reduced symptoms, some were capable of working. But they needed vocational training, counseling, and support in living with HIV. Social stigmas needed to be addressed.

More recently, the AIDS fallout has presented another difficult situation. The AIDS crisis of the late 1990s cut a swath through an entire middle generation of adults. Grandparents or other extended family members took in many of the children whose parents died from the disease. But now with these older relatives passing away, the challenge is, what will happen to the children, many themselves born with HIV?

Institutional care may be the only alternative in many situations, though it is widely recognized to be a less-preferred way of caring for orphaned or abandoned children. But with the likelihood of more children needing orphan care, we recognize the need to develop some way of evaluating and comparing the effectiveness of various types of programs. It is something we are working on.

I also saw how AIDS challenged the tendency to offer standardized and programmed responses to problems ("This is the way we do things.") in southeast Asia while I was with Tearfund. Along with several international NGOs, we were involved in some prevention and care programs in the region when we observed a disturbing trend.

The prevalence of the disease could be tracked along the route of a new highway being constructed through the Mekong Valley, up from Thailand to southern China. As the construction sites moved forward, truckers and commercial sex workers accompanied them, and AIDS cases mushroomed. Together with the other aid groups working in the area, we began talking about how we might switch our geographically based efforts for a more fluid approach, addressing the source of infections along the path of the newly constructed road and targeting the sex workers and their clients in an awareness-and-prevention campaign.

I was reminded of this some years later when Geneva Global began working on anti-human-trafficking issues in India. We also began to follow the trade routes, the roads and railways by which child workers were being transported. This meant developing trans-local initiatives and bringing together organizations from different jurisdictions, even linking activists and campaigners on each side of the India-Nepal border for the first time.

HOW CAN A PROSPECTIVE DONOR FIND OUT MORE about an organization that might be reticent to talk about failures or mistakes? Foundations may provide assessments of groups they have previously funded. Then there are private consultants who can make inquiries on your behalf. There are also giving circles and philanthropic networks where you might be able to talk informally with other donors about their experiences.

Some will tell of having been courted hard when they first expressed an interest in supporting a certain endeavor. But once they had signed the check, they found people at the organization less available, or they were not informed when funds were redirected for one reason or another.

While openness to questions is a sign of the health of an organization, so is openness to suggestions. Too often, in my mind, organizations get complacent and assume that, just because someone has been concerned about a particular issue in the past, that's all that interests them, so they keep bringing similar funding opportunities to the donor's attention.

But donors with an interest in a particular issue or a specific concern might prompt an organization to develop a new program and think outside the box. The donor-organization partnership can lead to exciting new initiatives.

Sometimes they even spring from a donor. That happened with a successful real-estate businessman who was concerned about the problem of piracy off the coast of Somalia. He started simply wanting to end a wrong by curbing the criminal activities estimated to cost billions of dollars annually. But as he researched, asked questions, and learned more about the issue, he began to see it in broader terms. The result was that he helped establish a foundation focused on job creation in Somalia, providing young men there with an alternative to piracy.

This kind of progression happens often as donors learn more about needs and opportunities. They start with a concern or a question that crystallizes over time into a project they want to support. An important part of that process is identifying the level of risk they are comfortable with. They have to decide what sort of social return they are looking for and then determine what level of risk they are willing to be exposed to in trying to reach that goal.

Recognizing that smart investment involves diversification, we encourage donors to consider getting involved with different kinds of projects. Some may be solid, dependable, and steady, with years of proven results. Others might have higher stakes, with innovative approaches to long-standing problems.

Take the current efforts to develop a hookworm vaccine. More than fifty million dollars have been given to developing a solution that would provide immunity against infection by the parasite, which is a leading cause of maternal and child morbidity across large parts of the tropics and subtropics. Though there are promising signs of progress, there is no guarantee that researchers will be successful. But if they were to be, it would be a major health benefit to almost six hundred million people.

We see more appetite for risk taking and bold gambles from people in the digital world, where they have embraced language that echoes our approach at Geneva Global. In Silicon Valley, they talk about "pivoting," which means attempting something and then refining or redirecting as they see how things go. We're all familiar with software beta testing, when an initial version is rolled out and improved upon as a result of feedback.

It's a much more positive attitude—one that encourages innovation and experimentation with the aim of getting better rather than just keeping the status quo. It gives people freedom to dream big while recognizing that not every idea will be a winner.

We've had our own share of flops along the way. We had planned a company that would offer philanthropic travel for prospective donors to provide them with exposure to the international-development sector. Another initiative involved an independent online database that graded the effectiveness of developing-world NGOs.

Neither idea took off as envisaged, but elements of both have been woven into other things we have done, as we have pulled useful lessons from the exercises.

It's all a bit like flying; no airplane flies directly to its destination, instead continually making small adjustments to allow for weather, traffic, and turbulence. In the same way, we've done our own course corrections as we've set our sights on reaching higher elevations.

LOCAL IMPLEMENTING

ANYONE WHO IS INTERESTED IN MAKING A DIFFERENCE in the world will have heard the advice, "Think global, act local." It's a sound strategy: remember the big picture, but start by doing what you can where you can. The two must go hand in hand for long-term change to occur.

However, when it comes to international issues like poverty and disease, we need to redefine just what we mean by "act local." From years of traveling to crisis spots around the world, I am convinced that the greatest impact is made when local community groups, rather than international organizations, carry out projects. Significant and lasting change is more likely in the hands of local people.

There are exceptions to this, of course. And I am in no way minimizing the remarkable work being done by foreign individuals and groups. In some situations, such as a natural disaster, there is no choice but to look to outsiders because the local infrastructure may have been obliterated, and those working in the area could be among the victims themselves.

At times, the scale of need is such that only a massive, international response beyond the scope of local groups can hope to make a difference, whether it's the aftermath of a tsunami or a large-scale vaccination effort. The most recent Ebola crisis in west Africa is a good example of where large, international organizations play a pivotal role. Some local groups simply do not have the man power or the organizational know-how needed to successfully manage big and complicated projects.

Sometimes local organizations' effectiveness is limited, not by any lack of their own, but because they are subject to governmental and administrative pressures that could not be exerted in the same way on an external body. What am I referring to? Everyone working in international development knows that corruption is just a part of the system in some places.

I remember my introduction to this reality in Liberia, even before being asked for bribes at checkpoints. I'd tasked a local member of our Medair team to go and buy some motorcycles for health workers in the hinterland. He came back, grinning wide. He had found a really good deal with someone who was going to give him a motorcycle, too, he said.

He was crestfallen when I told him we couldn't do that. He didn't understand when I told him that it was bribery. For him, it was just the way things were done there. "Their motorcycles are all right, and they are going to offer me something, too," he reasoned, "so why don't we go with them?"

Sad to say, the development world can be fertile ground for grafters, tricksters, and fraudsters. That is just one of the reasons we emphasize due diligence ahead of time and careful monitoring during projects.

Even those safeguards aren't always enough, however. Having researched one program well, we encouraged a donor to help fund a sizable school for orphans and vulnerable children in a west African country. It seemed to be an innovative program; in addition to offering an education, the school partially subsidized its operations by growing maize on the property.

Then we began to hear disturbing rumors about the headmaster—reports of erratic behavior and claims of sexual abuse. Deeply concerned, we instructed our program director to make sure no more funds were distributed until we were able to investigate further. But it was too late; the latest transfer had just been made. Though part of our processes required two signatures to withdraw funds at the other end, the headmaster had bribed the bank, hired armed bodyguards, and gone on the run with the cash.

We had no choice but to call in the authorities. Thankfully the man was arrested in due course, but the money was never recovered. Worse, the program was set back by the negative publicity. And I had the unpleasant task of telling our client that his thirty-thousand-dollar gift had been misappropriated.

This happened despite our best efforts and someone on the ground close to the situation. The potential for similar situations increases exponentially when there is no local presence. One wonders whether the allegations of abuse that surfaced at the school for disadvantaged girls that Oprah Winfrey set up in South Africa would have occurred had there been more effective local monitoring.

Most people in the development world don't like to talk about these kinds of missteps because they fear it makes them look bad. We certainly don't enjoy having to admit it on the rare occasions when things do go wrong, but we believe it's an important reality that needs to be faced. There are people out there who will try to take advantage of us, whether we are seeking to better the lives of others or ourselves. And not only in other parts of the world—remember Bernie Madoff?

Though philanthropic money is unfortunately misused from time to time, I remain persuaded that the possibility of misappropriation by local groups is far outweighed by the likelihood of the greater impact they can have. When you look at other development efforts from an investment mind-set, local organizations will nearly always produce a greater return on what is given to them.

Having said that, there are still times when I would recommend someone support an outside agency over a local group—such as when natural disasters strike, there is a problem of huge scope, or when programs require very technical knowledge. If they are not able to adequately learn about the community-based groups and agree on appropriate benchmarks, then I would advise someone to give their money where they know they will be sure of some results.

WHEN I THINK OF THE ADVANTAGES of working with local community organizations, my mind goes to the hardscrabble outskirts of Mexico City. One of the ten largest cities in the world and with a population of around twenty million, the Mexican capital lures countless people from rural areas with the promise of a better life.

For many, that never becomes a reality. They find themselves caught in the sprawling slum communities that ring the city and eking out an existence in desperate circumstances. It was here, in the slums that cling to the ravines in the Jalalpa and Presidentes districts on the western side of the city, that I met Saul and Pilar Cruz when I went to see how Tearfund's support was helping them. Over the course of more than two decades, this remarkable couple has effected change in a way no external effort ever could have.

A clinical psychologist, Saul might have pursued a career in private practice and ensured his family a comfortable life as part of the country's wealthy elite. But, determined to help those less fortunate, he and his wife chose a different path. Everyone told them they were crazy, but they went ahead anyway, explaining that they wanted to help some of the people in the slums.

The Cruzes were told they could have some land on which to establish a small community center at one of the local rubbish dumps. Their first task was to clear the plot of refuse so they could put up a small building from which to serve the area. Outsiders were viewed with suspicion; there, drugs, prostitution, and other crime were so rampant that even the police thought twice about going into the neighborhoods.

Violence wasn't the only threat. Raw sewage flowed into the open water running through the center of the ravines, where garbage was scattered indiscriminately. Heavy rains that would cause mudslides could easily wash away the fragile shanty homes thrown together on the slopes. Deaths from disease and accidents were frequent.

The Cruzes began simply, providing a place for children to go after school and starting homework clubs. The assistance was welcomed cautiously by parents aware of the importance of education in giving their children some hope for a better future. Next the Cruzes and their volunteers began to offer some vocational training for the boys that had fallen out of the school system.

In due course, the Cruzes actually moved into the area, making their home among the people they were helping, whose initial wariness was incrementally overcome. Those working with the Cruzes's nonprofit project, Armonia, which means "harmony" in Spanish, became aware of other needs they could never have discovered without being so well accepted.

One was the financial and social burden for the many couples in the neighborhoods who were living together but not legally married—in many cases not by choice but because they could not afford the various legal fees. In a strongly Roman Catholic country, such domestic arrangements were heavily frowned upon, and there was a considerable social stigma. In addition, the lack of official paperwork made it difficult for people to ever escape the area, even if they could come up with the financial means. Without proper documentation, it was impossible to apply for certain jobs and for housing and the like. Children born to unmarried couples could not get a birth certificate, limiting their future opportunities.

Troubled by these obstacles, Saul began arranging mass weddings. He would pay an official to come in and officiate at a ceremony for twenty or more couples at a time, throwing them a joint celebration at the community center. Not only did this open some new doors of possibility, it also gave couples who had been together for many years and raising families a new sense of dignity and a greater measure of respect and acceptance.

Over the years, Armonia's work has expanded in scope and scale. The Cruzes set up a health clinic and persuaded some middle-class doctors from another part of the city to come and start holding a clinic two or three times a week. Then they offered free dental care. They expanded to provide community programs in other parts of Mexico City and even other parts of the country. Teams of international volunteers now support the programs.

Key to Armonia's success has been its acceptance by the local community, which would likely not have been achieved had it been seen as an external program. The Community Transformation Centers at the heart of the programs are established through a three-part investment—a grant, a loan, and the local community's contributions—ensuring long-term buy-in.

All these efforts have led to other developments that are improving the lives of people in the community. Through answering countless individual needs and crises, the Cruzes became the people on whom others would call for help in the middle of the night. Armonia helped foster and develop a previously absent sense of community. That, in turn, gave people a voice they had not had before, leading to further change.

Concerned about the dangers to children in some of the open caves in the area, parents and others came together with the support of the Cruzes and were able to persuade local authorities to take steps to reduce the danger. Negative attitudes toward the authorities began to change as people began to see that they could have access to people in power.

What had been only a hopeless, downward spiral is now being transformed slowly into an upward, virtuous circle that offers hope and then finds ways to build on it.

IT'S HARD TO IMAGINE any international organization being able to develop the kind of program the Cruzes have. There are several benefits from partnering with community organizations.

First, they typically have a better sense of the realities of their community's needs. They have usually been established in a particular area in response to a perceived need. They have been working there, at some level, often long before the situation is brought to the attention of the wider world.

Often a visionary, charismatic leader, like Saul Cruz, has founded them and gathered around him or her others drawn to making a difference. They are passionate about the issue, immersed in and accepted by the local community, and many times have turned their backs on what could have been potentially lucrative careers to try to make a difference. To this end, they are less susceptible to accusations of only being there because they are getting well paid—accusations I faced in Liberia—than are Western workers.

Because they are embedded in and embraced by the community they are working with, leaders of local organizations are better positioned to leverage volunteer help from those they are serving. Indirectly, this means that they are able to generate more outcome from any income they receive.

The costs of funding local organizations are usually lower than for outside groups. While no one is going to become wealthy working in the development field, international groups typically pay more than their community counterparts. One unfortunate consequence of this is that they can draw local staff from other, smaller, local organizations, indirectly weakening these groups and their efforts. The fact that the INGO staff may be nationals means they might be accepted by those they are working among more than outsiders, but the group they represent is still not likely to be accepted in the same way that an indigenous organization is.

This may sound unkind, but there's a simple litmus test—just look for what happens to property and equipment when law and order break down. Chances are that the vehicles you see on the news, stolen or burning, and the buildings being looted are owned and operated by big outside groups. People tend to think that there's plenty more money where that came from, so it doesn't matter what happens, whereas they are more protective of those they consider part of their community.

It's also worth noting that, in times of disaster or trouble, local organizations don't leave. I'm not criticizing foreign workers for departing when things get too dangerous; our Liberia team evacuated when the risks became just too great to justify. But those we left behind kept things going.

The Liberians we had been working with might have chosen to flee across the border, too, but some of them stayed. Several of the men we had trained kept the revolving medicine fund we had established running for another two or three years as the country descended into further chaos. They could easily have taken the remaining money from the bank account in Cote d'Ivoire and run, but they decided to remain and keep serving their people. Two out of the three of them died during the ongoing violence.

When the people see an organization as essentially an external initiative—even though some of those staffing it may be from the local community—there just isn't the same sense of ownership or responsibility. That's just human nature, frankly; we so often divide ourselves into us and them.

I was surprised, though, how this sort of attitude can be found even when there is clear-cut evidence of benefit. I remember hearing about a successful health program in Namibia as its seven years of considerable overseas funding and operation was coming to an end. The project had resulted in significant improvements, and the government was in a position to assume the ongoing costs. But when I inquired of officials and community leaders whether they would be keeping the initiative going, I was told, "Oh no. That's got nothing to do with us."

This exchange reminded me that there's an important emotional dimension to successful international development. While people in need are grateful for help, of course, they still want to maintain their dignity. They don't want to be simply objects of charity. They want opportunity and responsibility for their own lives.

When funding for a particular initiative ends, the entire program usually doesn't grind to a halt if it is being run by a local organization. The scale or scope may need to be reduced in the event of less money, for sure, but often those involved find some way to keep things going. Indeed, this is actually a pretty good rough measure of the true and lasting value of an initiative.

The importance of sustainability as a goal in any kind of change program—from the environment to education to health—is being increasingly recognized. Supporting community organizations helps meet that goal indirectly by encouraging and equipping them to be more efficient and effective. Groups we select commit to organizational training and development as part of receiving a Geneva Global–recommended grant. That means the group is more experienced and operationally better situated, even when the funding ends.

This is a second way a donor can measure the success of supporting a program. Your money has bought two things: There is the specific activity that has been made possible— the number of wells that have been dug or the number of children who have been fed or vaccinated. But then there is indirect impact of that investment—how the organization may have grown, its people trained, leadership matured, and horizons broadened. How much more might they achieve in the future because of what they learned and how they developed from your period of support?

Working with local organizations does present its challenges, of course. Doing true due diligence overseas can be time- and labor-intensive. There are also cultural differences to overcome. We have learned that what we are told by some of our partners in the field isn't always the way things really are, but this doesn't necessarily mean they are trying to hide anything from us. It is just part of the different way in which they view the world, relationships, and endeavors. In the West, we have been trained to ask straight questions and expect direct answers, but in many parts of Asia and Africa, it is culturally important to save face, both yours and the other person's. That can mean people sometimes tell you what they think you want to hear—not because they are trying to deceive you so much as they don't want you to be disappointed.

Like the time we were overseeing an education project in Rwanda for a client who was funding a building program at a secondary school. We were a little concerned that things seemed to be running behind time, but the progress reports we got assured us that everything was on track. We were told construction was completed, the equipment was on its way, and the students were due to arrive any time.

Still, something didn't seem quite right. We sent one of our local representatives out to the school to check. There were no finished classrooms, no equipment, just some walled rooms—a few still without ceilings.

As we investigated further, we learned what had happened. Because of the recession, the price of cement had skyrocketed, and the funds we had originally designated for the project were no longer enough. So work just halted, and rather than tell us what had happened, the organization tried to pretend everything was fine. Once we had all the facts, we were able to revise the project, find the extra funding needed for circumstances recognized to be beyond anyone's control, and see it successfully completed.

It would be easy to look at situations like this and be critical. There can be inefficiency and waste. Some groups do seem to duplicate the efforts of others while important things just get overlooked entirely. I've known businesspeople who see philanthropic work up close and shake their heads and dismiss those involved as well-intended amateurs—do-gooders who mean well but don't really know how to run things.

I've certainly come across ineptitude and incompetence in my travels, but for the most part, the men and women I've met who are involved in helping those in need are skilled and dedicated. The simple reality is that doing good—which essentially means trying to bring about social change of some kind—is often way more complicated than running a business. There are so many more factors, players, unknowns, and variables.

The occasional problems don't dissuade me from preferring local groups to INGOs and other organizations; they just reinforce for me how development work is so complex, requiring not just goodwill but good systems and procedures for extending it.

STRATEGIC PLANNING

THERE IS A LOT OF BLACK-AND-WHITE THINKING IN BUSINESS and leadership. You only have to look at some of the best-selling management books to see how they often advocate either-or approaches: you can have this or that, but you have to choose between the two. The trick is to be decisive and go for one or the other, they insist. Saying yes to this means saying no to that.

It's often the same in international-development circles. You can have scale, or you can have sustainability, the thinking goes. Scale invariably comes with the weight and wealth of big international nongovernmental organizations and other large groups. They have significant numbers of people and levels of resources to apply to needs. They have experience. They can make a sizable difference.

They also usually have a more programmatic-based approach to issues that can ignore local complexities and nuances. That's just the reality of big organizations. They need systems and protocols, which are set far in advance and tend to run a certain way and only a certain way. And, as I have observed in the previous chapter, their impact is less likely to be as long-term and far-reaching as that of local community organizations.

These smaller groups, however, are oftentimes dwarfed by the size of the challenge. They may be best placed to go deep, and their programs are likely to continue to make an impact long after any outside funding may have ended. They just do not have a very broad reach.

This tension frustrated me for years as I saw how much more effective development efforts would be with a "both-and" result, delivering both scale and some measure of sustainability. Then I revisited an old adage that helped me visualize how it might be possible to deliver both.

I am sure you have heard the saying about how giving a man a fish feeds him for a day, but teaching him to fish feeds him for a lifetime. It's practical wisdom and the heart of much good work around the world. Fishing lessons don't just equip people, they empower them too. They provide dinner and dignity.

But then I thought, What if those individual fishermen represented organizations, and what if they interwove their lines? They could create a net that would catch more fish than any of them could on their own. What if we tried to bring a number of local organizations together to address an issue in the same area? Might they be able to achieve more together than any could alone?

The answer has been a clear yes. One of the first places Geneva Global saw it realized was in Ecuador, where, by joining forces while maintaining their own identities and special areas of interest, around a dozen community-based organizations have made a major impact in the area of human trafficking.

Lured by the false promise of well-paid jobs in other parts of Latin America or even the United States and Europe, children and teenagers in rural parts of the country were especially vulnerable to traffickers looking for young prostitution and slave-labor candidates. With one in five Ecuadoreans living well below the poverty line, such enticements were all too attractive to youngsters and their families in places like Ibarra, a border town close to Colombia.

Though prostitution is legal in Ecuador at age eighteen, some of the girls recruited to the sex industry—thriving under the guise of cafes, karaoke bars, and even auto shops—were as young as twelve and thirteen.

Brought together strategically by Geneva Global, the small Ibarra-based organizations working to combat this illegal trade found a united voice that the authorities could not ignore. As a result, they were able to press for changes in the national law, which were enacted and aimed at cracking down on the traffickers. This was in addition to their individual efforts, which included preventive education and leadership training in schools and counseling and rehabilitation for victims.

Encouraged by this success and other examples, we began to wonder what might happen if we took a similar approach on a larger scale. One of the first things I had done upon joining Geneva Global was establish a task force to review what and how well we were doing. One of the strong recommendations that came back was to stop funding small projects somewhat randomly in different parts of the world and to begin to cluster them more strategically for greater impact.

That, together with our experiences in places like Ibarra, led to us working with the Legatum Foundation to develop what we have called a Strategic Initiative model to take on some fairly ambitious challenges.

We began looking for issues or places where we might be able to bring together a wide range of local organizations in a concerted effort to make a major impact. Not just programs that would be welcomed and result in some difference but a united front that would bring about significant, lasting change. Maybe not wipe a problem out completely but certainly achieve enough so that people would acknowledge a clear before-and-after difference. A tipping point.

That requires focus. A laser rather than a sunlamp. But many times, it seems to me, development programs have emphasized the reach rather than the depth. Treating half a million people in scattered locations for a certain disease sounds more impressive than effectively eliminating it among a much smaller population. But is it necessarily the best way to spend the money that is available?

As we developed our first portfolio of Strategic Initiatives, we realized that the success targets we were setting required a strong cluster of effective local organizations. They would need considerable funding over three to four years and typically needed to be focused on a single sector, such as education or health. By bringing organizations together,

113

we hoped to be able to eliminate a lot of duplicated efforts, thereby increasing overall efficiency and effectiveness, and provide for better management of the individual programs.

We launched our first series of Strategic Initiatives in 2007, using this clustering approach. Among the issues we addressed were education needs among the children of migrant workers in China and an alarming rise in the HIV infection rate in Odessa, Ukraine's third-largest city, which threatened a major AIDS outbreak in the country.

After three years, we conducted a detailed analysis of the twenty-two Strategic Initiatives comprising 150 individual projects in nineteen countries. The overall number of projects that our thoroughgoing review assessed to have "achieved" or "overachieved" turned out to be 10 percent higher than for previous, individual, nonclustered programs we had been running prior to 2007.

In the process, we discovered a number of ways we could improve things even more, but we knew that we were onto something. One clear lesson was the importance of being geographically focused; when projects are scattered over too wide an area, it is difficult to monitor them closely or really measure their cumulative effect.

The Strategic Initiative approach might be best pictured like an orchestra. Each player brings his or her own instrument and skill and concentrates on the score he or she has been given. Individually, some of the chords and notes may not be very striking, but all together as an orchestra and under the right conductor ensuring everyone is in tune and on time, they can create a symphony.

The reality is, however, that many organizations are soloists—or "siloists." Historically, there has been a lot of silo thinking in international development. People are seen one-dimensionally—as AIDS patients or at risk for malaria or some other concern. It's an understandable approach, but it falls short. Providing improved education is all very well, but how much have we really helped if a child gets good schooling but is suffering from intestinal worms and can't concentrate on lessons?

We need to take a more holistic view, looking not just at individuals but the environments—the ecosystems, you might say—in which they live. Having studied the bigger picture in this way, it then involves seeing how contributions by different groups and agencies can contribute to the whole.

AMONG THE PLACES I'VE SEEN, firsthand, the results of this kind of comprehensive, collaborative planning is in Patna railway station near the capital of the eastern Indian state of Bihar. With a population of over two million, the teeming city is one of the oldest continuously inhabited places on earth, dating back almost three millennia.

It is also a hub on one of the main arteries of a major scourge of the twenty-first century: human trafficking. The Global Slavery Index estimates that there are nearly thirty-five million adults and children enslaved around the world and that around sixteen million are to be found in parts of India, Nepal, and Pakistan.[1]

The busy Patna station is one of the junctions from which children lured into and procured for slavery from northern India and across the border in Nepal have long been dispatched across the country.

They may be headed for domestic servitude, forced to work long, grueling hours. Or they could be taken to construction sites, farms, or manufacturing plants, where they are locked into their sleeping quarters at night, effectively imprisoned.

Little hands are in high demand by carpet makers because they are especially nimble and adept at handling the heavy weaving looms. Sadly, young bodies are prized, too. Many of the girls taken south with the promise of work as, say, a maid are likely to end up in brothels. They are candidates for the sex trade when as young as six or seven—boys, too, sometimes.

---

1. The Global Slavery Index 2014, accessed December 2, 2014, http://www.globalslaveryindex.org/.

Then there is even a black-market trade in children's organs, providing the likes of a healthy young kidney to someone rich, sick, and looking for a donor.

The children pass through Patna station and others like it in the hands of traffickers who have made false promises to the parents. Visiting rural communities where families endure grinding poverty, they talk of great opportunities for good work in safe places. Sometimes they will even persuade the parents to pay them for their so-called help in securing one of these ghost jobs.

Not all parents swallow the lie completely, but even if it may be only half true, for some, the prospects can seem better than the reality they know. Desperation can cause people to turn a blind eye.

But now there are more allies who have both eyes open, like the porters I met in the railway-station lunchroom. They told me how, along with some of those on the platforms selling food to travelers, they have been trained to spot suspicious movements and alert authorities to potential traffickers. They are part of a whole network of ears and eyes looking for unlikely family groups traveling together along this trafficking route.

On its own, this volunteer watch would be an admirable but inadequate enterprise, like patching a hole in a leaky hosepipe when there's water gushing out of the standpipe head, too. But as part of an integrated effort that is looking at the problem strategically to reduce the source, restrict the flow, and rehabilitate those who have already become victims, this one intervention is having a marked impact.

By applying a comprehensive, "orchestral" approach to the issue of human trafficking in this part of the world over the past few years, we have seen greater effectiveness. For example, we have been able to help coordinate and amplify the work of twenty-eight different organizations on opposite sides of the India-Nepal border. Though these organizations shared a similar goal of reducing modern slavery and some were separated by only twenty miles or so, many of them had never met. So we brought them together as part of a strategic and comprehensive antislavery program and made sure they understood each other's mission, initiatives, and areas of expertise.

Nepali children rescued from the slave routes in India would often then find themselves caught in limbo. Because they had been brought into the country with false or no papers, they didn't have the documentation necessary to enable them to be repatriated to Nepal. With groups in India and Nepal now collaborating, this Catch-22 situation is being resolved, and children are getting to go home.

The twenty-eight organizations are focusing on preventing Nepalese and Indian men, women, and children from getting snared into trafficking, conducting rescue and rehabilitation interventions like the work in Patna, and working with transport police, magistrates, and the legal systems in both countries to provide more protection for vulnerable people exploited by organized criminal networks. By helping each of the organizations realize how they fit into a larger effort, we have seen increased cooperation and better coordination from those involved. Like twenty-eight instruments in an orchestra, each of these organizations plays its part, leading to much greater effectiveness overall.

APPROACHING ISSUES IN THE COMPREHENSIVE WAY we have developed offers the potential of great impact, but it isn't without its challenges.

There's the matter of bringing different organizations together collaboratively in the field. Groups working in the same physical area or within the same sphere of concern do share a level of collegiality, of course, but there is also a measure of competitiveness, as I have previously observed. There is only so much money out there in the donor world, and everyone wants funding for his or her program. That means differentiating yourself against the others.

Even when there is willingness to team up, it takes a certain amount of time to go beyond polite acknowledgment of other groups to actively engaging with them. That is one of the reasons we have found it important for our Strategic Initiatives to be funded for several years—at least three. Another factor is that it often takes more than one year to begin to see impact at the level we are looking for.

Our field managers wear many different hats in the course of a project—one of the most important being that of a diplomat to bring the various leaders of different organizations together for a common purpose.

Over the course of time, we have found that groups begin to gain a greater respect for each other and look for ways they might additionally work with or support one another. They talk about things they might do together outside the initiative in which we have brought them together. The net we have helped weave will remain in place long after the initial funding has been exhausted.

One example of this from the first Strategic Initiatives we directed can be seen in Malawi. The original program had involved bringing together a wide range of different churches in a coordinated response to the country's AIDS crisis that had left one million children orphaned—one in every fourteen of the population.

For three years, the Legatum Foundation funded an effort that saw local congregations putting aside their denominational differences to join forces and care for AIDS sufferers, look after orphans, and provide prevention education, vocational training, and some microloans.

The project itself achieved, according to our analysis, which was good news. But what was even more encouraging was what I discovered on visiting Malawi a few years later, after our AIDS program had ceased. A couple of the mills that had been established as an income-generating component of the program, where villagers would pay a small fee to have their maize ground into flour, were still running as self-sustained ventures.

Having seen success with the consortium approach in one area of need, we wondered whether we could apply it to another. In 2013, we resurrected these groups, repurposing and redirecting them to run early-childhood-development (ECD) programs being funded by Oxford University Press. Through this initiative, children are being fed, socialized, and prepared for school for an annual per-child cost that is about the same as a typical monthly child sponsorship run by large nonprofits. On the shores of Lake Malawi while touring a maize grinding mill that had originally been established as part of the earlier AIDS initiative, I saw a wonderful working example of sustainability and local ownership. It was now a business that paid for the children's lunches in the ECD program.

Part of the process of fostering the potential for this sort of ongoing cooperation involves developing what we call a community of practice. This requires regular meetings of representatives of all those who are part of a Strategic Initiative, usually about every three months. They spend a day or two together, reviewing progress, discussing problems that may have arisen, celebrating successes, and seeing which areas need attention.

When you bring a dozen or twenty groups together around a common cause, they have different areas of focus and different skills and weaknesses. There will be advocates and activists, program organizers and practitioners, leaders and line personnel. Some groups turn out to be exceptional at the hands-on end of their work but wanting when it comes to accounting. Others may have terrific organizational systems in place but are weak in their actual client service.

When we discover the areas that need strengthening, we arrange for one group that has some expertise in that particular aspect to help others by running a training day or arranging for a staff visit. If there is a wide enough need, we will bring someone in from a local consulting company to offer coaching and help. We call this capacity building; we're not just enabling the different groups to operate today, we are helping them do so more efficiently and effectively in the future.

All this requires a certain amount of openness and flexibility from the organizations we partner with. It's an attitude we are looking for from the get-go. When we identify an issue we believe would make a good target for a Strategic Initiative, we invite relevant organizations to come for an initial in-country meeting, where we set out our philosophy of approach. We are not looking for detailed grant applications from them at that stage. Rather, we are looking for a willingness to be part of something bigger than themselves, which might require some flexibility and adjustments on their part so that they better fit with the broader initiative.

This exploratory phase is an important one, where local organizations help shape the actual strategy. We don't go into a situation assuming we have all the answers. Our first main interest is in asking the hard questions that others may not have posed.

It's not uncommon to find that—because different organizations are working independently, for the most part, in an area—they are sometimes not so much solving a problem as simply pushing it along or creating another one somewhere else—another example of unintended consequences. Without standing back to look at the big picture, it's hard to get a proper perspective. It's like pressing down on a half-filled balloon: you can flatten the part you put your hands on, but the air just pops up somewhere else. You need multiple hands, each applying pressure in their own space, to bring things to bursting point.

Obviously the kind of comprehensive approach we pursue in Strategic Initiatives necessitates a significant investment of time and money in planning and preparation. But our analysis of what has been achieved points to the fact that both are well spent, producing deeper and longer-lasting returns. And the bold nature of the approach is appealing to some donors who are willing to take a certain amount of risk to make a big difference.

WHILE BEING GREAT ENTHUSIASTS for working with community-based organizations where possible, this is only part of what contributes to really successful strategic planning. Just as we advocate both-and thinking for getting scale and sustainability, we also believe that a program will be most effective through a combination of "bottom-up" and "top-down" elements that reinforce and mutually leverage each other's activities. An example is our creation of a Thailand anti-trafficking program in the seafood and shrimp industry. The community-based projects would be augmented by national advocacy funding and supply-chain analysis to put top-down pressure on policy makers. The evidence the local organizations supply about the trafficking on the fishing boats and in the processing sheds provides vivid examples, testimonies, and data that back up the pressure applied at the national level.

This bottom-up, top-down approach relates back to the *Star Trek* chessboard I had in my Tearfund office. Playing with the traditional set of pieces across three boards arranged vertically and being able to move up and down across boards introduces a lot more complexity, which is symbolic to me of the complex social change we are trying to execute around the world.

Imagine each of the three chessboards as different levels of interaction in the real world. The bottom layer is the local community context—Patna railway station or out-of-school children in rural Ethiopia. This, we try to address utilizing a strategic plan of clustering local community actors. The middle layer is the regional, or sometimes national, level. Here is where our Ecuadorian partners fit in by creating a national advocacy program to change the child-protection laws. The third layer is the international or global arena. In Tearfund, as part of the Jubilee 2000 international coalition, we achieved significant developing-world sovereign debt reduction, and nations were able to spend the dividend on education and health initiatives. In east Africa, millions more children were able to go to school for the first time.

Another example of operating at this third level is what happened with a handful of neglected tropical diseases. A concerted effort of governments, NGOs, the scientific community, and pharmaceutical companies has meant that donors provided nearly 1.35 billion NTD treatments in 2013, compared to 995 million treatments just two years prior.[2] While much more needs to be done, this international coalition has galvanized global actors toward making sure these tropical diseases are neglected no more.

We often see these three levels interrelating in world events. September 11, 2001, shows us how local buildings in two US cities were attacked and led to regional instability in the Middle East for over a decade. We live in a complex, interconnected world. The social problems we seek to solve are complex, three-dimensional, interconnected, and long-term. Thus, it stands to reason that the solutions we have to employ need to have the same characteristics. We need strategic planning based on a sophisticated understanding of the local, regional, national, and international dimensions of the challenges we face. We need to construct well-crafted, three-dimensional responses, combining top-down and bottom-up elements. And if possible, we need to stick with a situation long enough to make a real difference. That seems, to me, to be the difference between doing good and attempting to change something permanently.

---

2. T. Salaam-Blyther, "Progress in Combating Neglected Tropical Diseases (NTDs): U.S. and Global Efforts from FY2006 to FY2015," *Congressional Research Service*, accessed December 2, 2014, http://fas.org/sgp/crs/misc/R42931.pdf.

DELIBERATE MULTIPLYING

THE IDEA OF LEVERAGING PHILANTHROPIC GIVING, of making the money you give to help others work harder isn't new, of course. Matching grant campaigns have long been a part of the charitable world and can be used effectively. But Geneva Global is unusual in the way we put so much focus on looking for that extra bang for the buck.

We are indebted to Legatum for their determination in getting the most impact from their philanthropy and consistently pushing us to think through what might be the great in a program, not just the impact for the direct beneficiaries. The great comes in many different forms but always takes the form of deliberately multiplying the impact of the investment. It can involve leveraging other people's donations, changing policy, proving a new and innovative model or tool, working with academic partners, magnifying the collective voices of our implementing partners, planned replication of the program elsewhere, or scaling up the program in situ. These multiplication elements always lead to more positive outcomes for not much more than the price of just doing a good program.

It is an integral part of our approach, from the what-if question that sparks initial research into a potential project, through its planning and implementation, and then onto its completion. We want to know what we can achieve that is beyond the specific goal of the individual program. Is there some way this initiative can be used as a springboard or an incubator?

Maybe helping organizations in their efforts to counter human trafficking will lead to them bringing about a change in the law, as happened in Ecuador. Perhaps supporting efforts to improve educational levels by helping children who have missed out on schooling is a model that could be replicated in others parts of the world, as happened in Mali, or alternatively act as a model to redesign the way children in regular African primary schools are taught. We are after multiplication or acceleration of some kind.

It's true that some additional results from initiatives can't be predicted. But if you don't plan for multiplication, it probably won't happen. It requires conscious intent in the designing of the philanthropic endeavor.

One way we have done that is by taking on academic partners in our Strategic Initiatives. When we looked back at the end of our first three years of programs under this clustered approach, I was excited by the results. We'd clearly improved our impact. I was proud of what we had achieved and eager to share the information with others. But I was a little disappointed by the response we got to our reports. People were not as impressed as I thought they should be.

Then I recognized that they only had our word to indicate how well things had gone. Perhaps they were exercising the same kind of caution to our claims as we advise people to show for other organizations. Fair enough; the Internet has not only made the world smaller, it has made it flatter in at least one way. Someone with a well-designed website, a collection of eye-catching images, and a few heart-wrenching stories can make him or herself look great, even if there is no way of measuring the true impact.

Clearly we needed some independent verification of what we were saying. So we have selectively added academic partners to our Strategic Initiative approach, inviting researchers known already as specialists in their particular fields to independently evaluate what we are doing.

Foundations have long turned to educational institutions in a similar way, but typically to examine an initiative once it has been completed. Where we have differed is by asking academics to be part of the program from the start. Their questions and contributions can help identify things that need changing or improving as the project goes on.

Being open like this requires both confidence and humility: confidence that our work stands up to scrutiny and the humility to know that we won't always get things right and can learn from others. We believe that the kind of transparency required in having academic partners is attractive to potential donors. And when the academic partners write favorably about our projects, they become megaphones for our message: independent affirmation is the best kind of public relations.

Looking for the right institutions to partner with has taken us around the world. For help with the Speed School initiative in Ethiopia, we turned to the Centre for International Education at the University of Sussex in the United Kingdom. The people there are considered world experts in accelerated learning. Focused on studying education and development in developing countries, the center has carried out extensive research and consultancy for governments, INGOs, foundations, and development agencies.

The Kilimanjaro Centre for Community Ophthalmology in Tanzania came alongside in our work in the Valley of the Blind in neighboring Zambia, offering technical expertise for the treatment drive aiming to eliminate trachoma cases. The survey they carried out independently assessed trachoma levels to be high enough for the region to qualify for donated drugs from an international medicine bank, which reduced operational costs.

The Center for Global Health and Development at Boston University (BU) has been attached to our orphans and vulnerable-children initiatives in Ethiopia, while the William Davidson Institute at the University of Michigan—known for its expertise in public-health supply-chain logistics—has been part of evaluating an integrated rural health program in Namibia. This program seeks to improve poor health levels and services by bringing together all those involved in the health sector in a pilot project in the country's northern Ohangwena region, and was also studied by the Wharton Business School's Global Consulting Practicum at the University of Pennsylvania.

This kind of rigorous academic scrutiny comes with a cost. Often, around 10 percent of a project's funding has to pay for the research and analysis, but we are convinced that, in larger programs with the right circumstances, the results are well worth the investment—both in improvements to the specific program and in how its results can be replicated elsewhere.

Our association with BU has also led to something that could, in turn, have a big multiplication effect. When AIDS devastated Africa in the 1990s, it decimated the middle generation of mothers and fathers. Thankfully, the continent's extended family culture meant that grandparents or other relatives took in many of those orphaned.

But, as I have already noted, these older caregivers are now passing away themselves. A demographic time bomb is ticking on the continent. There are now twelve million parentless children living in sub-Saharan Africa alone. The extended African family is close to reaching its breaking point, leaving orphanages as the next-best solution. As I have also acknowledged, institutional, residential care of this kind is widely accepted to be a less desirable option, but in many places, it is becoming the next-best alternate choice.

With that in mind, it is increasingly important to ensure that only the best providers of orphan care are funded in the years ahead. Through our relationship with the BU team, we learned that they had been working on a tool for measuring the effectiveness of orphan programs in India and realized that this was something that could be developed for wider use.

With funding from the Legatum Foundation, we have initiated research that examines thirty-six orphan programs in Ethiopia, which can be cross-referenced with child health-outcome data. The study is still being finalized as I write, but the MODE (Measuring Organizational Development Effectiveness) assessment tool has already been adopted by some organizations for use in evaluating programs. We believe that the money spent on this will, in due course, ensure that much more money spent elsewhere is better used.

MULTIPLICATION CAN BE MEASURED in a number of different ways. It might be scaling up the original program, recruiting other organizations to the platform that has been created, or replicating the initiative in another region or even country.

Another way we gauge our effectiveness is in the social change that results. This brings us to an enormously sensitive but important issue in international development: the question of cultural sensitivity. There's nothing worse than an ignorant foreigner with all the answers—or who at least thinks he or she has them.

I am reminded of the nineteenth-century journalist and author G. K. Chesterton's famous definition of a tourist: someone who laughs at everything, except the jokes. It is an insightful description of someone who goes abroad with blinders on. They don't understand anything they see or hear, so they laugh at it all. But because they don't understand anything, they can't laugh at the real jokes.

At the same time, I fear that, too many times, the need for appropriate cultural sensitivity has been hijacked by political correctness. In the world of international development, that means that sometimes root issues do not get addressed, challenged, or even discussed because there is concern about offending someone.

But if true change can only come when we affect not only someone's conditions and circumstances but also their thinking—the forces beyond their control that may be part of the reason for the difficulties they face—that can mean challenging cultural norms and values.

This is a very delicate area, naturally, and another reason we always look to work closely with nationals and local organizations. But there are some things that are simply wrong, however much they may be a part of a local culture, enshrined through generation after generation.

Female genital mutilation is wrong. Handicapped babies should not be abandoned or allowed to die because they are not good enough. Girls and young women should not be forced into prostitution. Impoverished families should not be held as slaves to make other people rich.

These and many other situations of human suffering in the world today are flat-out wrong. Both the factors and the values that perpetuate them need to be challenged and changed.

It is not for us to do this in an imperialist way, of course. There is a difference between empire building and nation building. One is imposed from the outside, and the other is composed from within. We look to help equip and encourage those who are part of those communities and cultures and already hungry for change.

It is understandable that some groups might want to avoid swimming in these kinds of tricky waters, but we believe it is vital for true, lasting change to come about. It is not something to be undertaken lightly, however—a fact that was underscored for me one time as I sat on a rickety chair in a small village outside Varanasi, in India's northern Uttar Pradesh state.

I felt a bit self-conscious, as I stood out not only because of my height but due to the fact that I was the only person sitting on a chair. One of the few around, it had been given to me as a mark of respect for our organization, while everyone else in the community sat on the ground. The leaders told me a remarkable story.

They recounted how, for generations, families in the area had been held in bonded servitude to the owners of a local brick kiln and factory. Young children were forced to work alongside their parents, all held in debt by exorbitant loan rates that could never be repaid.

Then workers with an Indian anti-trafficking organization one of our clients was funding came to the village. They learned of the situation and began to talk with the community leaders about how they might begin to organize themselves and push for better terms and conditions.

This kind of militancy is high-stakes activity. Someone in another village who had tried to press for change some years earlier had been attacked by the kiln owner's private security force and thrown into the kiln fire. In another situation, I heard a stone-quarry owner ordered all the homes of his bonded workers burned to the ground when they started to express dissatisfaction. A young boy died in the flames.

So it was only cautiously that the people of the village began to meet and discuss how they might work for a change in their circumstances. Encouraged and coached over a period of a couple of years by our partners, the villagers finally came to the place of putting their feet down. They formed a Community Vigilance Committee, and they presented a collective face to the kiln owner, refusing to work for him any more unless things changed.

This was a major step, considering they were in a remote area far from the protective presence of local police. The people were risking their livelihoods and their lives. But their gamble paid off. The brick-factory owner reluctantly agreed to concessions that improved the families' situations.

But the story didn't end there. Someone pointed out to me a well-dressed man standing off in the distance, twenty feet or so from the edge of the group gathered around me. The man was a relative of the brick-kiln businessman, I was told. He had been sent to keep an eye on what was happening in the village because, emboldened by what they achieved for themselves, some people from the community had been contacting other villages in the area to pass on their experiences and successes.

They were doing so under the constant threat of reprisals, a sobering reminder for me of the fact that, in the West, helping others find freedom may cost money, but in many parts of the world today, it may still cost people their lives.

LOOKING FOR THE MULTIPLICATION FACTOR as we do doesn't appeal to all donors, we recognize. Some have a more conservative approach to their philanthropy, as they do in their regular financial dealings. They prefer a more certain, if perhaps smaller, return than some who are comfortable with accepting more risk for the chance of a higher return.

But in the same way that financial investors are advised to consider diversifying with different levels of risk for portions of their money, we encourage donors to consider supporting Strategic Initiative programs across a range of risk levels. Because we keep close track of goals and benchmarks, if a particularly high-risk initiative isn't working out as hoped, we can agree with the client to halt that effort and reallocate its portion elsewhere if need be.

I would never unduly criticize anyone for having a more risk-averse philosophy of philanthropy; after all, they are still doing good. But I would want to challenge them to consider looking for more return and want them to know that, for those who are willing to take some chances in the pursuit of greatness, it can be an exciting and fulfilling journey.

This came home to me in a deeply personal way when I returned to Namibia for the first time in more than thirty years. I had left the country having been awakened to the ugly reality of inequality and injustice and having made some efforts at effecting change—though, in hindsight, paying some of the disenfranchised Bushmen to cut a road by hand was truly just scratching the surface.

Three decades later, I was there to take a personal look at the way we were partnering with the Legatum Foundation in an attempt to radically improve the health of rural populations in the country's remote north.

Home to two-thirds of the total population, the area suffers high levels of poverty that have been exacerbated by recurrent flooding and an influx of people fleeing problems across the border in neighboring Angola. Diarrhea, malnutrition, and respiratory conditions are rampant and, though treatable, often end in death—as they do for millions across Africa.

Ohangwena, the district in which our study and pilot program is based, is underserved with health facilities. There are just three district hospitals and two health centers, plus some clinics and basic health outreach locations for a population of over 225,000 spread over four thousand square miles.

It is no secret that many different aspects keep people healthy and productive—nutrition, hygiene, safety, and so on—and when thought of and planned for in a comprehensive manner, a community can provide better, holistic care for its residents. Maximizing resources is an especially critical factor when they are limited in proportion to the need. But so far, no one has really come up with an approach that is sustainable and replicable.

Our Rural Health Integrated Network Initiative has brought together an unprecedented range of participants. Among those committed to being part of the project are several INGOs, representatives of other groups focused on specific disease initiatives, foundations, and national and local Namibian representatives from health care, education, the police, and hospitals.

The first phase has centered on identifying some of the holes in the existing net of services. For example, some of the basic health-care locations are understaffed, so people make a difficult journey by foot to seek treatment, only to find that the specific drugs they need are out of stock. This sort of practical scheduling challenge is typically foreign to those of us in the West, but it is an everyday reality in parts of the world where money is short, data is often missing or late, and the infrastructure is poor. And it can have serious implications for the health and future of the country.

"I'm sick of people coming to my hospital at the last minute and basically presenting themselves at such a late stage that it's often impossible to help them," one senior medical leader in Ohangwena told me in exasperation. "And then the newspapers blame us that too many people are dying in our hospital."

Comprehensively addressing this kind of challenge will involve equipment, logistics, and training, but our first steps have been at a more fundamental level. We are trying to be a catalyst, bringing ordinary people together with health professionals, schools, and government ministries and encouraging them to believe that, together, they can improve their community's health. Breaking down the problem and identifying the various systems at play echoes the approach often used when I was working at Lucas Engineering & Systems, and we've seen the benefit from this methodical thinking.

A community-wide "health-for-all" campaign has been organized, with another aspect of the initiative working in schools to address the rate of teen pregnancy, which is among the highest in the Ohangwena region of Namibia. The core team of leaders has already led and launched a large-scale advocacy campaign and three micro projects without the need to wait for outside funding. Among the micro projects are a school health project tackling hygiene, sanitation, nutrition, and teenage pregnancy, and a regional health-data management-and-analysis initiative.

What has been especially encouraging so far has been the high level of interest in participating in the project from the local leaders even though we were not in a position to offer any grant monies. As the program develops, we anticipate more individuals and organizations will see what is being achieved and will want to be part of it, and hopefully this includes more local funding.

Early indications have been good. Different stakeholders in the country have told us that they have never seen such openness to cooperation before. One foreign governmental development agency frustrated by its inability to make an impact in the Ohangwena region after some years working there has indicated it wants to switch from unsuccessful attempts to run its own health program to supporting one of the micro projects Geneva Global has been able to initiate.

We won't know just how well the Namibian program is working for several more years. But if this Strategic Initiative is successful, it will not only have a notable impact in that part of the country but can then serve as a model for similar programs across the nation and even in other parts of the continent.

It was special to be back in Namibia and see so much wild land still untamed and appreciate again the wide, empty skies and the rugged natural beauty. It brought back many memories, and I was grateful for those early experiences that had been so pivotal in my life.

But what was even more personally fulfilling was to spend time with the Geneva Global program manager responsible for getting it all launched on the ground in Namibia, my daughter, Alex—who now goes by Lexi—just a few years older than I had been when I was first in Namibia.

It reminded me of another aspect of truly effective philanthropy: maximizing impact for the long term will be seen only if we are open to working more collaboratively across groups and generations.

ACTIVE COLLABORATING

DEVELOPING GENEVA GLOBAL'S APPROACH TO PHILANTHROPY has been a journey of discovery. Like following a trail, sometimes you only see the direction you need to take when you round a corner or crest a hill.

That was the case as we sought to cluster local community-based groups together in the search for scale and sustainability. It seemed to make a lot of sense at the field-based end of things, but then I began to wonder whether the same idea might be beneficial at the donors' end, too.

What if we could bring individuals, foundations, and funding agencies together more intentionally? Multiple funding sources for projects is nothing new, but supporters tend to have their own separate relationship with the group they are helping, with no connection between themselves. It seemed to me that there could be some advantages in having different donors actively work together, in tandem, rather than just in parallel.

I had been struck by a conversation with representatives of one of the world's largest private foundations. They told me of their frustrations at not having all the money they wanted to be able to achieve all their goals. If they couldn't find all the resources they needed, surely others had the same challenges, I reasoned. What more might they do together? We found the opportunity to test this theory in Rwanda and Burundi.

Massive funding has rightly gone into developing treatments and finding a cure for the likes of AIDS, malaria, and tuberculosis, which are scourges of the developing world. But there are other diseases that also cause tremendous problems, like trachoma, the eye infection that plagues Zambia's Valley of the Blind.

It is just one of several neglected tropical diseases that affect over one and a half billion people.[1] Half a million people die each year as a result, while many others suffer pain and long-term disability.[2] Infected children suffer malnutrition, which, in turn, impairs their physical and mental development.

Infected flies spread river blindness. In addition to transmitting malaria, mosquitoes can spread lymphatic filariasis. Attacking the lymphatic system, this parasite is responsible for elephantiasis, which can make limbs swell grotesquely, causing disability and social stigma. Freshwater snails carry schistosomiasis, also known as bilharzia. Untreated, it can lead to bladder cancer and kidney, liver, and spleen problems. Hookworm, roundworm, and whipworm—often grouped together as soil-transmitted helminths—cause internal obstructions and lead to stunted growth and impaired functioning.

Together, these five diseases ravage large parts of the world where they thrive because of poverty, unclean water, poor sanitation, and overtaxed health-care systems. Yet there is a fairly simple and inexpensive treatment that can all but eradicate them. And the long-term impact in tackling them is very significant. A study by Michael Kremer, the Gates professor of developing societies in the Department of Economics at Harvard University, found that simple deworming of children in Kenya improved not only their health but, in turn, their educational achievements, job prospects, and quality of life. All for a little less than fifty cents per child per year.

Learning of this major possible impact in 2006 from a *Financial Times* article by Andrew Jack, Alan McCormick, Legatum's managing director, asked us to organize a concerted attack on four of the five diseases in Rwanda and Burundi—lymphatic filariasis not being prevalent there. Typically, the diseases had been tackled separately, in the

---

1. "Uniting to Combat Neglected Tropical Diseases," *Delivering on Promises and Driving Progress: The Second Report on Uniting to Combat NTDs*, 2014, accessed December 2, 2014, http://uni-tingtocombatntds.org/report/delivering-promises-driving-progress-second-report-uniting-com-bat-ntds.

2. *Neglected Tropical Diseases*, Centers for Disease Control and Prevention, 2014, accessed December 2, 2014, http://www.cdc.gov/globalhealth/ntd/.

usual silo approach, but for a few years, scientists had been advocating a new strategy in line with our thinking—one that meant drugs could be given together and up to all five diseases treated at the same time, at cost savings around 40 percent.[3] The Legatum Foundation-initiated response was the first joint private philanthropic initiative of its kind and scope.

Over the course of four years, more than nine million people in the two countries were treated twice annually with NTD drugs at a total cost of less than eight million dollars. Recognizing that treatment alone would not be effective, these mass drug administrations were coupled with prevention-education programs. Helping to keep costs down was the fact that the pharmaceutical companies were willing to donate the drugs for free, and the governments mobilized children to attend clinics and schools in a Mother-and-Child Health Week across the two countries.

It is one thing to try something ambitious, but it's the results that are most important. Following rigorous standard medical-evaluation guidelines, we concluded that the four-year initiative saw major strides forward in the two countries' public-health standards. In some of the four pilot sites in Burundi, prevalence rates of schistosomiasis dropped from a high of 50 percent to below the World Health Organization's 10 percent threshold of concern. The total cost of this effort was around thirty cents per person per year.

Encouraged by these results, the Legatum Foundation wanted to take things to the next level and turned its attention to the rest of Africa. But its funds alone were clearly not going to be enough.

Alan and I began to talk about what might be done. We reflected on how capital-investment funds work in the business world, creating a platform for others to join, and wondered whether a similar approach might be applied in the philanthropic world. The result was the END (Ending Neglected Diseases) Fund, launched in 2011. It is a private

3. M. Brady, P. Hooper, and E. Ottesen, "Projected benefits from integrating NTD programs in sub-Saharan Africa," *Trends in Parasitology*, 22, issue 7 (July 2006), accessed December 2, 2014, http://www.cell.com/trends/parasitology/abstract/S1471-4922(06)00121-8?cc=y).

philanthropic initiative aimed at raising one hundred million dollars to deal a deathblow to the diseases that have disabled and killed so many.

Incubated by Geneva Global, the now-independent group is currently carrying the baton from Burundi and Rwanda to more than fifteen countries across Africa, as well as India and Yemen. Geneva Global and Legatum have been joined by hundreds of other donors, including the Bill & Melinda Gates Foundation, the Campbell Family Foundation, Dubai Cares, and the Global Network for Neglected Tropical Diseases in an unprecedented private-sector cooperative attempt to control and eliminate the most prevalent NTDs within a decade. As of 2013, over fifty million people at risk of NTDs have received treatment. And more funders continue to join the cause.

In its early days, Geneva Global managed the technical and logistical aspects of the END Fund on a contract basis. In 2012, the new group hired its own CEO. Alan and I serve on the board, and, while Geneva Global continues to provide some programmatic services, the initiative is now fully independent.

HAVING SEEN THIS KIND OF COLLABORATIVE APPROACH prove fruitful in one area, I immediately began to wonder where else it might work. My thoughts turned to an issue that has drawn worldwide attention in recent times: human trafficking.

The terrible injustice of men, women, and children being traded like livestock is something of a different one in the philanthropic world. Usually some people somewhere have been working away quietly to address or eliminate some threat, like an endemic disease or regional poverty, before it gains public attention. In due course, philanthropic concern and funding follows.

With human trafficking, the reverse has been true. Over the past few years, there has been a great deal of media coverage and public discussion on the issue, but in terms of the vast need and challenge, the level of on-the-ground activity has been quite small.

Bringing together peer philanthropists in the same way that the END Fund rallied those concerned about neglected tropical diseases, the Freedom Fund launched in 2013, with Geneva Global having again played a background catalytic role. Unveiled by former president Bill Clinton at his Clinton Global Initiative gathering in New York City, the Freedom Fund brings the Legatum Foundation together with Humanity United and the Walk Free Foundation to raise one hundred million dollars for smart antislavery investments worldwide.

Such a huge problem is daunting—where to start? No one really knows how many people are caught up in bonded servitude and prostitution and other kinds of exploitation. The estimates have run from twenty-one to thirty-six million people.[4] Whatever the actual figure, it represents a big challenge, a multibillion-dollar shadow economy whose beneficiaries will not easily cede their interests.

One of the problems of this kind of illicit industry is that fighting it becomes a bit like a frustrating version of Whac-A-Mole. Attack its visible presence there, and it goes underground and pops up somewhere else.

For instance, in Nepal, some traffickers have switched or even expanded their trade routes. Instead of transporting people across the border to India, where they have been coming under closer scrutiny, some have been redirecting those they recruit to the Middle East and even Europe. The traffickers arrange for work visas, but the migrants are often conned into exploitative servitude situations instead, working as domestic help or as construction workers in harsh situations with no way out.

Geneva Global was contracted to lay the early groundwork for the Freedom Fund, identifying several geographical hot spots around the world where we might focus early efforts and learn how bringing organizations together in our clustering approach can effect change.

---

4. Free the Slaves, 2014, accessed December 2, 2014, https://www.freetheslaves.net/page.aspx-?pid=375.

One of those target areas is in northern India, where we first began to realize the results of a clustering-type approach to change through our earlier projects. It's not unusual to find a few groups working together, to some degree, in different areas of need around the world, but the India-Nepal Human Liberty Initiative has almost thirty groups committed to cooperative action—an unparalleled number—focused on prevention, protection, and prosecution.

In line with our hopes for momentum and multiplication, some of these organizations have joined forces in their own initiative, founding the Indo-Nepal Social and Anti-Human Trafficking Forum. Bringing together groups working on both sides of the border, the new network aims to improve communication and cooperation so that rescue and rehabilitation efforts are more effective.

Meanwhile, one of the groups a Geneva Global client has funded in Varanasi, India, as part of this Strategic Initiative has recently achieved a breakthrough that could prove to be significant in bringing child-trafficking operators to justice.

Workers with the nonprofit group Guria had become exasperated. They would provide police with details of people involved in child-sex trafficking, but after the operators were arrested, they would be let out on bail. Then the traffickers would intimidate witnesses and drag out court proceedings, with cases sometimes taking up to six years to come to trial. Meanwhile, their illicit trade continued.

To break this logjam, Ajeet Singh, Guria's founder, filed a public-interest litigation. As a result, the Indian Supreme Court ruled that those arrested for trafficking minors for commercial sexual exploitation should be denied bail—a move that has increased the prosecution rate, will accelerate cases through the system, and make it more likely witnesses will testify, all improving the chances of conviction.

There is no reason that the collaborative model of the END Fund and the Freedom Fund could not be extended to other areas of concern. We are looking into the possibility of developing a similar Speed School–based fund that would seek to improve educational opportunities across Africa along the lines of the program in Ethiopia.

But beyond that, what about slum transformation as a significant focus, perhaps? The possibilities are considerable as people come together. I'm reminded of Harry S. Truman's famous quote: "It is amazing what you can accomplish if you do not care who gets the credit."

This principle drives another area of Geneva Global's work that goes on largely behind the scenes. We work with individuals and foundations that want to broaden their impact by bringing together peer organizations or other philanthropists to either co-invest in their philanthropic work or complement their funding to build a more holistic response. For example, a philanthropist investing in services to small-scale farmers may seek out partners who will invest in irrigation infrastructure.

Geneva Global helps make that connection by identifying potential partners, conducting a landscape analysis of who else is giving in a given region or sector, developing strategies for outreach to potential partners, and creating communication materials that are targeted for private philanthropists and foundations. For example, a billionaire philanthropist recently came to us for help in broadening support for his goal to use tablet technology to improve educational opportunities in Africa and how to engage other private donors in this issue.

We're seeing a trend in donors seeking out this type of advice on how to engage with other donors—and where there are opportunities and competitors. We are often quieter about this work as we understand that partnerships—and more broadly, relationships—are rooted in mutual trust built over time. While we provide the tools and strategies to identify and more effectively engage with potential partners, it is our clients who reach out and make the connections.

BRINGING PEOPLE TOGETHER to make a collective impact is becoming a popular topic in philanthropy circles and industry publications, such as the *Stanford Social Innovation Review*. In the United States, philanthropists are coming together with local NGOs, government, and other actors to tackle complex domestic challenges with comprehensive, inclusive strategies. We have been doing the same since 2007 and finding equally encouraging results on an international stage. But it is not without its challenges. After all, while those who are willing to cooperate at this kind of level let go of some degree of ownership, they don't give up everything. People don't usually write large checks and then just forget about them. Nor would we want them to; after all, our whole aim is to see donors actively engaged in their giving.

Having said that, newcomers to the world of philanthropy are sometimes surprised by the degree of caution and even suspicion that can exist between different organizations and groups addressing a common cause. They expect competition in the business world, but there seems to be the general expectation that, when it comes to doing good, people should just put their differences aside and work together.

In the same way that some people wonder why there are so many different denominations when Jesus talked about all his followers being one, others are astonished to discover how many different NGOs exist—somewhere in the region of thirty thousand in Rwanda alone, by way of example. That is one for every four hundred men, women, and children in the country.

I knew from my experience in getting the Micah Challenge, the Micah Network, and Integral off the ground that everyone involved needs to feel that they aren't just helping someone else but that they are benefiting as well. But finding that sweet spot between independence and collaboration has proven to be harder work than we had expected.

The END Fund was set up so that major participating groups each got offered a place on the board. That meant they not only had an active role in steering the movement but were given open access to all the financial details. They were also able to choose to which part of the initiative their money was directed.

With governmental and multilateral funds, all the money typically goes into a central pool, but we knew that this would never work in the world of private philanthropy. By giving END Fund member groups ownership of their part of the whole, as we did, they could detail to their own stakeholders to which parts of the overall project their investment was going specifically.

One thing that did catch us off guard was that each member body had its own reporting expectations. We had assumed that we would be able to provide them with standard annual reporting, but it turned out that each had slightly different requirements and wanted them according to *their* calendar year, not ours. This meant more organizational work than we had anticipated, but the investment is still worth it in terms of the greater returns that will come from the END Fund's collective impact in the years ahead.

While I see great potential for collaborative approaches like this, we're not suggesting they are the only way ahead. For me, they are a welcome tool in the toolbox needed to fix a broken world. We are not trying to replace everything that has gone before; indeed, one of the concerns I have is that much development work over the years constantly gravitates to new ideas, much like each season brings about fashion trends.

There was a time when microfinance was seen as the big new answer, offering financial capital to poor communities. I certainly welcome that, and microloans have proven very successful in some situations, but they are not the sole solution. In some circles, that emphasis has given way to the more recent interest in social-impact investment: doing good while doing good business. There are exciting possibilities there, without a doubt.

But the world is always going to be too complicated for a one-size-fits-all solution. That is going to mean we will never have it all figured out, and we will have to keep being open to new ideas and combine them with older ideas we know work. I know that is hard. Personal change is challenging and difficult. While looking for ways to change the world at large stimulates me, I can be less keen when it comes to my personal world. Just ask Anna how I react when I find out she has bought me a different kind of shower gel! We all get comfortable with what we know and dislike having to adjust.

New ways of looking at and doing philanthropy are like that too. Not long ago, I spoke at a conference, where I presented some of the thinking behind another new idea we have. I talked about bringing together strategic granting and impact investment, mixing donor money and business capital, and pointed out how much traditional granters and newer impact investors had to offer each other. That talk was warmly received, but I heard about two other sessions on the same topic at the same event that ended in much rancor, with the new business philanthropists essentially accusing traditional donors of having failed to make a real difference in the world, despite all they had spent, and just perpetuating some of the problems with their outdated ideas. The old-school supporters, in turn, dismissed their critics as naive business newcomers who didn't have a clue what they were talking about, being out simply to make money under the guise of helping others and, as capitalists, the reason for so much inequity in the first place.

My hope is that those on differing sides of the debate will be able to put aside their personal convictions long enough to at least consider that the others may have something to contribute: collaborative thinking and then, perhaps, collaborative action. One thing is sure, effective philanthropy tomorrow will not look like it did yesterday, nor necessarily even as we think it should from today's vantage point.

FORWARD LOOKING

BASEBALL PHILOSOPHER YOGI BERRA was right when he said, "It's tough to make predictions, especially about the future." One thing I have learned about forecasting what is to come: it's easier to do in hindsight. There are just too many variables to be too definite about the way things are going to be in the days ahead, especially in the area of international development. That is why I get nervous when I hear people talking too specifically about what lies before us.

There are meteorological, political, cultural, and economic unknowns. A drought or a government coup, and another nation may be plunged into crisis. But change doesn't have to be for the worse, of course. One area that continues to develop rapidly, offering great hope for development, is technology.

It is interesting to see how mobile-phone capabilities have enabled huge advances in Africa, for example. Much of the continent has leapfrogged into the computer age, going straight from limited access to communications to instant wireless connectivity. Mobile banking is commonplace in many parts, with some organizations making microloans available by cell phone.

Others are using them as part of systematic health campaigns. One of the challenges, historically, in seeing widespread health advances has been to ensure that drug regimens tackling the likes of tuberculosis are completed. It's not uncommon for people to start to feel better when they begin a course of medication and then stop taking what has been prescribed, thinking they are better even though the condition has not been completely eradicated. The patient then is vulnerable to drug-resistant diseases that are much more difficult to cure. Following up on hundreds of thousands of people has understandably been beyond the abilities of governments and NGOs.

But now, a text-messaging program exists that reminds people to take their daily medications. If they don't text back within a certain time to confirm they have complied, a second message is sent to someone the patient has identified as a backup. You're going to be sure to take your meds if your mother comes around to check up on you. For some conditions, doctors are able to make basic diagnoses and recommend treatment on the basis of photos sent by mobile phone, allowing for earlier intervention in areas where there is no ready access to specialist help.

So I am hopeful as I look ahead, especially as we refine our methodologies to ensure that we maximize every dollar that is given. But I think it's important to make one clarification as we consider the future. That's when we talk about financial sustainability—a phrase tossed around a lot in development circles. The problem is, there is no real agreement on what it means, just that it must be a good thing.

Newcomers to international development assume that financial sustainability refers to projects that can financially continue after the initial funding stops. But most of us who have been involved in this realm for any amount of time know that's unrealistic. Unless another donor comes in to replace the funding, the project activities will diminish drastically, at best.

Most grants, by definition, cannot be financially sustainable vehicles because—unless they have some sort of revolving-fund component, such as my drug program in Liberia—they use up money rather than generating it. In philanthropy, you are giving money away, and when it is spent, it is gone. One of our clients, a keen supporter of Geneva Global's investment mind-set, jokingly refers to his philanthropic giving as "capital destruction." And he's essentially right.

We can make the money work as hard as possible, though, as in our early-childhood-development program in Malawi, which incorporates flour mills as a way for the community to become more self-sufficient. Or as in the Liberia-style revolving drug fund as part of our Valley of the Blind initiative in Zambia that we estimate will extend the program for another two years without the need for extra outside money.

There is also a somewhat intangible form of sustainability we look for—the learning and organizational development a group experiences during the time it is being funded, which hopefully leaves it stronger and more capable, even when the grant has ended.

That is why much of what we are doing in our projects is seeking to find ways to improve conditions and circumstances so that people can continue without outside help. But that is not always possible. There are some things that need to be done that will never be capable of generating income; they are simply an expense. These are the areas where there simply is no financial return in bringing about social good. Anti-trafficking activities, for example, do not present a revenue model. These sorts of situations will continue to need grant support. It is granting as a public service.

Charitable organizations, pretty much by definition, are reliant on people giving them money so they can continue what they are doing. That is why you come across hugely frustrating situations in the development world, like relatively new ambulances sitting unused because the original project that provided them did not include funds for maintenance or a way of ensuring that the need for future upkeep and care was taken into account.

The new generation of philanthropists that is emerging may have some of the answers we need to these kinds of challenges in pursuing true financial sustainability.

Some are approaching the idea of doing good from a different mind-set, integrating social good into their business practices and principles. This is opening up possible solutions in areas we might not have expected previously.

That's why the concept of impact investment is so appealing. Loans and equity to for-profit enterprises— businesses—that provide socially useful products and services have a lot to offer poor communities. And businesses can be sustainable. By way of example, the growing concern for the environment has led to some people giving money to help

151

subsidize the development of energy-efficient cooking stoves. These cut the need for charcoal burning, protecting the environment while helping families.

Ultimately, good business development for a healthy economy is the long-term answer to poverty. That is why it is important to help create an environment in which business can prosper. But in the short term, now, we have a duty to help those who, through no fault of their own, are caught in circumstances they simply can't extricate themselves from. We need to step in and, through granting, do what the free market can't.

One change I believe we will see in the future is a shift in the center of gravity of philanthropic giving from the West to parts of the world where the need exists. Since the country opened up economically, there is a new generation of wealthy businessmen and women and entrepreneurs in China, for instance. I was astonished to find that, within two years of China's allowing the establishment of private foundations in the country in 2011, around four thousand had been established. A similar thing is being seen in Africa and parts of Asia: people of means who want to help make a difference in their own part of the world.

What is going to be interesting and challenging but also potentially significant is bringing together all kinds of developmental aid in a united strategy, marrying philanthropy and socially responsible business. We have some ideas how that might work.

WE CALL IT THE INTEGRATED FUND. In some ways, it's a culmination of all we have learned to date, bringing those lessons together in a way that we hope will create a place of big change, to do not just good but great—to produce a tipping point.

What would that look like? Much of what we take for granted in the developed world: somewhere that people get to grow up healthy with the opportunity for an education that develops their individual abilities to their potential so that they can find productive work and enjoy a secure life.

That requires things that we can help provide, foster, and develop: education, health care, and economic development. But it also needs a stable government with which to partner at different levels.

Recognizing that there are multiple factors and players in such an initiative, the Integrated Fund concept is based on being capital agnostic—in other words, we don't care what kind of money is used to achieve the overall goals, just as long as it is the most effective.

This means we might offer grants where there is no revenue model, provide loans where recipients are able to make repayments, and even take out equity in social businesses. This blended capital—when strategic granting meets socially responsible investment—will be used to improve health, education, and economic conditions in a concentrated, focused area.

Grants and loans between thirty thousand and one hundred thousand dollars will be offered—larger sums than are typically offered by microloans but smaller than most impact investments. But it's the range of investment we believe is necessary to be able to effect change in really needy places. This seed funding will be buttressed by training and other business support that will bring new enterprises to the level where they can take on new staff and may independently attract further investors.

By concentrating on education and health, we will raise the well-being, productivity, and capabilities of the local community, creating a more educated, healthy workforce that will be more attractive to outside investors and fill the new jobs created. New jobs will, in turn, mean more money flowing into the local economy, allowing improvements to infrastructure and services. It is all part of the virtuous, upward circle we are looking to achieve.

Some of all this may sound rather familiar. That is because it bears some similarities to the Millennium Village Project launched by renowned economist Jeffrey Sachs (at Columbia

University) that has brought a concentrated, multipronged approach to dealing with problems that has seen some success in cutting child mortality, improving infant health, and increasing agricultural yields in parts of Africa since the turn of the millennium.

Where it has so far failed to produce greater results, in our view, is in tailoring its program to the capacity of the local community. While we agree that concentrated effort and investment is needed to see significant change, it needs to be applied at a rate that doesn't outstrip the ability of local organizations and systems to accommodate and absorb new practices and approaches. This means investing considerable time and attention on capacity building in the early stages, laying a bridge that will be able to carry the weight of change in the long term.

The Millennium Village Project also requires such a large amount of grant capital to be concentrated in a relatively small area that it is not really replicable. However, our Integrated Fund benefits from some of the other lessons learned to date through the Sachs initiative. We know that there needs to be enough flexibility within the program to allow for and to adapt to feedback from local community leaders and organizations so that the plan can be adjusted and refined as time goes by. Otherwise, you tend to end up with a solution that feels like it has been imposed by outsiders rather than one that is developed with their help.

With the Integrated Fund, we will be emphasizing a collaborative, cross-sectional approach that gives local stakeholders a significant role in the planning, development, and assessment of the program so that they do not view it as someone else's, as those I met in Namibia did.

Our most ambitious initiative to date, the Integrated Fund, has been developed in partnership with Capital for Good, an independent charity we set up in 2009 to facilitate philanthropic giving by foundations and individuals. The Capital for Good trustees have funded the initial research for the Integrated Fund, knowing that it is not something that will bring immediate results.

We think that it will take a decade or so to truly see what kind of impact is possible to achieve with a measured, multifaceted approach of this kind. The time frame is much longer than many philanthropic projects, which are often funded for two or three years, meaning it will likely appeal to a particular kind of donor.

Worth bearing in mind is that the longer the funding, the more money goes to the actual activity. In part, that is because there has to be a front-end investment in planning and setup. But is it also the nature of the life cycle of projects. There is always a period of getting up to speed in the beginning, ironing out kinks, and then a slowdown in the last few months as the funding starts to come to an end.

If it takes three months to get things going well at first and then there is a dip in performance in the last three months— when program staff may start looking for fresh funding or even for new positions for themselves—then half of a twelve-month program will be operating at less than optimum levels. If that same program is funded for three years, though, you have the possibility of two and a half years of high performance. Over a decade, there is even more potential for a good return on the investment.

In addition to extended funding, our Integrated Fund also needs the right test bed. It needs to be somewhere that has challenges, opportunity, and enough need to be able to measure and monitor legitimate impact, but not so overwhelming that the chances of success are minimal. With that in mind, we have turned to Africa and northern Uganda.

The Integrated Fund for Gulu focuses on an area of the country slowly starting to recover from years of violence and neglect, during which the infamous Lord's Resistance Army (LRA) terrorized the population. The group abducted around thirty thousand children, with more than one and a half million people displaced.

Some have slowly begun to return home to rebuild their communities since a cessation of hostilities agreement was signed between the government and the LRA in 2006. Now the Integrated Fund for Gulu aims to help accelerate that effort by supporting local businesses and organizations as they work together.

Over a ten-year period, the fund will help finance efforts in areas like education, small-business enterprises, and mental health care. Though 90 percent of those working in Gulu are employed in agriculture, the land is significantly underutilized, so one idea is the starting of a "machine bank" from which farmers can lease equipment to expand. Another focus of the fund will be to help address issues of emotional well-being; many people in the district witnessed brutality during the years of conflict or lost a family member to the violence.

Our hope is that, with all these facets, the Integrated Fund for Gulu will have an impact at such a scale that it will, in turn, attract other NGOs and agencies that can use what we have established as a platform on which to add and integrate their own contributions toward the rebuilding of the region.

NEW APPROACHES SUCH AS THE INTEGRATED FUND, the Freedom Fund, and the like are not change for the sake of it. They reflect a significant shift occurring in the world of philanthropy—one that the Chandler brothers were among the first to anticipate.

This trend is both cultural and technological. For many years, philanthropy was largely the province of the older generation—people who had made their money and wanted to use some of it to establish foundations that continued after they had died. Some of the largest foundations in the world today are the legacy of nineteenth-century wealth. Inherited money has been another major philanthropic source.

The Internet has changed things in many ways. It has brought the world closer to home for everyone. Awareness of global need can no longer be avoided or ignored, even if you want to. It is right there online, every day. The Internet has heightened a sense of interconnectedness—that we are all part of a global village.

The democratization of the World Wide Web has also fueled greater openness to cooperation and mutual interests. We live in the day of crowd sourcing and flash mobs, when people join forces to make information freely available to everyone—Wikipedia—or make people smile by singing the "Hallelujah" chorus in a mall food court. There is still a strong go-it-alone culture in the business world, but even there you will find greater openness to beneficial alliances.

The digital age has produced a generation that is more connected, more open to collaboration, and eager to do something now instead of waiting until some time in the future. Socially responsible business has become a welcome trend, though you have to look carefully here. There is a lot of chatter without real action, with some who are more interested in the public-relations benefits than the actual results.

Then there is the new community of people in business who want to spend some of their money on doing good now, even as they continue to build their brands and assets, rather than waiting until later when they are more established. Dubbed "philanthrocapitalists," many of these emerging business leaders see a natural affinity with the performance philanthropy model we advocate. People in the digital world, where they are constantly pushing into what is new and what might be, seem especially enthusiastic about innovative approaches to making a difference and some of the opportunities we present through Geneva Global.

Among those I have connected with is a successful Silicon Valley entrepreneur originally from India who wants to find ways to use new methodologies and technology to improve educational opportunities in Africa. We have also been in discussions with the leaders of a successful online gaming company interested in starting a philanthropic program and possibly even bringing development issues to the attention of their large gaming community.

In part, I believe this kind of interest is because of the entrepreneurial culture fostered by technology. Failure is almost acknowledged as a requisite for success, as the widely embraced pivoting principle illustrates. I have heard it said that some Silicon Valley–type investors won't look at an entrepreneur's proposals or recruit a staff member unless they've failed at something at least three times. They need to have had success, too, of course, but the idea is that if they haven't failed at something, then they probably haven't been thinking far enough outside of the box to truly come up with something new. This expansive philosophy makes us a fit when they are considering philanthropy.

Coming soon, too, is another shift that will likely have a big impact on how philanthropy is done—one of the largest wealth transfers ever seen in history. The West's baby boomers will be leaving the money they have generated to the next generation—children and grandchildren who are much more philanthropically, internationally, and socially aware because of the technology and global connectedness they have grown up with.

This generational change cannot be ignored by anyone who is concerned about changing the world for the better. The emerging generation simply believes it's their responsibility to leave the world a better place—even as they pursue their own goals and dreams—in a way that people of my age and older did not do to the same degree.

Additionally, we should acknowledge and commend the way present-day wealthy figures like Warren Buffett and Bill and Melinda Gates have served as role models for those wanting to use their money to make a difference. To date, more than one hundred billionaires have signed The Giving Pledge—a commitment to give away at least half of their wealth to charity—since the trio announced the initiative in 2010. Among those who have pledged are well-known names like Larry Ellison, Barron Hilton, Sheryl Sandberg, T. Boone Pickens, and Mark Zuckerberg.

It has been interesting to work with some clients who have noted the changing attitude toward wealth and philanthropy, seeing it as an opportunity not only to effect change in the world but also to strengthen their own families and pass on important values.

You don't have to do much more than glance at the news to know that large amounts of money can be a curse just as much as a blessing. Second, third, and further generations can struggle to handle responsibly what they are left. So we are seeing families approach philanthropy with twin goals for the world and for themselves.

There is a real interest in facilitating families by sitting together and trying to work out what they want to give money to and for everybody involved to have some sort of voice in the process. Philanthropy is seen as one of the positive things that can cement and build family trust and communication, as opposed to business interests that can so easily divide. To me, it's another example of the fact that, properly approached, doing good can never be bad for you.

The shake-up being experienced in the world of philanthropy is uncomfortable and can seem confusing for many, both the givers and the practitioners. Philanthropic giving and activity has been done pretty much the same way for the past half-century or so. But I believe that the changes we have seen and that are to come are to be welcomed for the way they demand more of everyone involved, from the donors to the doers, pushing us from being complacent in just doing good to looking for more ways to do good great.

ACTIVELY ENGAGING

FOR ALL THE EMPHASIS WE PLACE ON MEASUREMENT, metrics, projections, and performance, there is one important aspect of philanthropy that can't be tracked on spreadsheets or analyzed in a board meeting. It's what happens inside the person who is giving.

No matter how effective the program someone financed turns out to be, I don't think we have been entirely successful unless they have been changed in some way, too, as a result. I always advise prospective clients that in partnering with us they are embarking on a journey of discovery about themselves and the world.

If they are new to philanthropy, they can sometimes feel a bit overwhelmed by some of the ideas we present. I tell them not to worry, to start by following their heart, but to just be sure to bring their head along as well. We didn't develop our philosophy of performance philanthropy overnight, and donors shouldn't feel they have to be experts before they can start making a difference.

Americans are among the most generous people in the world, giving somewhere around three hundred billion dollars each year.[1] That is more than the gross national product of some 140 countries. But it's been well said that charity begins at home, and that is certainly where most of the US donations remain. Three out of every four foundation dollars go to domestic causes.[2]

There are many worthy domestic causes; that's certain, but at Geneva Global, our hope is that, while charity begins

---

1. *Giving USA 2014 Highlights*, Giving USA Foundation, 2014, accessed December 2, 2014, http://store.givingusareports.org/.

2. *Key Facts on U.S. Foundations*, Foundation Center, 2013, accessed December 2, 2014, http://foundationcenter.org/gainknowledge/research/keyfacts2013/grant-focus-geography.html.

at home, there is a place for international assistance. Once people have seen how they can make a difference here, we like to be able to show how they could multiply that impact several times over in other parts of the world, where the same dollars can go much further.

Some focus on domestic giving because they believe that's where they should. For others, it can be because they don't know of the opportunities overseas. And since 9/11, some have been leery about giving money in other countries out of concern that the money may fall into the hands of terrorists—a fear our stringent due diligence and monitoring can alleviate.

Though philanthropists develop different areas of concern, children are a common entry point to the world of giving. Their plight is so often our awakening to the vast need that is out there. There is something about the vulnerable young that touches a chord in all of us. We may think, rightly or wrongly, that adults have more responsibility for their circumstances, but we recognize that children are the victims of famine, abuse, poverty, and poor health through no fault of their own.

Through the years, I have witnessed more than my share of suffering, so I was surprised by what happened when I was visiting a refugee camp in Burundi many years ago.

I'd seen many starving children, just skin and bones. Then I came across a small three-year-old boy in the camp's malnutrition center. His belly was distended by kwashiorkor, a protein deficiency that causes the body to shut down. This little boy was near death, but the medical staff hoped that they might be able to save him with a simple porridge diet.

Despite the hope they offered, I found myself sobbing uncontrollably as I watched them care for the small boy. Later, wondering why this particular brief encounter had touched me so deeply, I realized that the infant was about the same age as my youngest son, Ryan, who was safe, secure, and well fed half a world away.

Having, perhaps, given money to support some sort of children's program somewhere, many people then begin to see some of the complexities of the problem. The children they are helping to feed are malnourished most likely because of inadequate education and poor local infrastructure, so while providing a meal today is important, something more needs to be done to break the cycle.

Realizing that creating social change is hard can be demoralizing. As can discovering that not everyone who claims to be doing good in the world is actually very effective, or perhaps even to be trusted. But for those who press beyond these sobering realities, the rewards are hard to measure.

In her famous book, *On Death and Dying*, Elizabeth Kubler-Ross identified the five stages of grief typically experienced by those facing the end of life—their own or a loved one's—as denial, anger, bargaining, depression, and acceptance. I have observed a common pattern in those active in philanthropy, which I describe as empathy, enthusiasm, disillusionment, determination, and commitment.

FIRSTHAND EXPERIENCE CAN BE AN IMPORTANT PART of the evolutionary process in philanthropy. We always encourage donors to consider visiting the programs they are helping to fund, rather than just relying on what they might be told in a report. There is something about seeing with your own eyes what your money is providing that cannot be compared.

Some supporters are reluctant to make these kinds of visits, fearing that they might seem patronizing or paternalistic. My experience has been just the opposite. Not only do beneficiaries not resent being visited, they actually welcome it. They are touched when someone gives of their time to come and visit, conferring a sense of dignity and honor, as well as a sense that they are valuable enough for someone to want to invest their days in, not just their dollars. Visits like this don't just give you a greater appreciation for the complexities of international development, they underscore why it is important to keep working for change even in the light of challenges and setbacks. You see it in the faces you never forget.

I still remember meeting Clarissa in the mid-1990s while visiting an AIDS care program with my then twelve-year-old son, Jonathan, in Zimbabwe that Tearfund was helping to support. An attractive, shy teenager, she was the oldest of three orphaned siblings. Their parents had both succumbed to AIDS, leaving Clarissa to raise her two smaller brothers—just one of countless child-headed households.

Our funding was enabling local churches to send out home-based caregivers to help orphans like Clarissa cope. They paid for schooling and provided some food and support. Perhaps it was because she was about the same age as my daughter, but I was drawn to Clarissa in the same way I had been to the little boy in the Burundi refugee camp. I asked her the names of her brothers and how she was coping.

I returned home encouraged that we were able to help youngsters like Clarissa, and I was eager to know how she was doing when I went back to the area a couple of years later. I spoke with the program director, describing Clarissa and her two brothers. How were they all, I wanted to know?

"She's not part of the program anymore," he told me.

My heart sank as I heard that Clarissa and her brothers had been separated and farmed out to different family members. As happens not uncommonly, relatives had begun feuding over who should inherit her parents' meager estate, and Clarissa had been caught in the middle. She had ended up moving in with and marrying a much older man because it seemed like the only solution.

Clearly this is not a success story. But it continues to motivate me to want to be part of making the world a better place for all the Clarissas and all their brothers.

I am also encouraged when I think about the many people we have met and have heard of whose lives have been changed for the better because of our efforts. Urmila was just fifteen when she was lured from her poor home in Nepal with the promise of a well-paying job in India. She found herself effectively sold to a circus, where she was forced to perform dangerous acts.

After four hard years, during which she was made to work up to eighteen hours a day and beaten for the smallest mistake, she managed to escape. But she was shunned when she tried to return to her home community before finding her way to Share and Care. This community-based organization one of our clients helped fund as part of a comprehensive anti-trafficking initiative in the area offered counseling and encouragement, and Urmila was able to establish a new life for herself. Today she is an active part of a local women's group, warning others about the dangers of trafficking.

Martha seemed doomed to a life of grinding poverty with her illiterate parents. Limited in their income potential by her father's blindness, the family scratched out a living by growing food on their small piece of land in the Ethiopian village of Morocho Shondolo, supplementing their earnings by selling some of the milk produced by their only cow.

Busy helping care for her family and fetching water, Martha had no time for school. When one of our Speed Schools was set up in the area, she was encouraged to enroll and surprised the instructors with her abilities. Finishing Speed School, she was placed in a fourth-grade class in the government school system, only to be promoted to the fifth grade just a few weeks later as her new teachers realized how well she was doing. A star pupil, now she has earned the support of her parents, who see hope for her future in pursuing education.

While we believe in looking hard at the numbers in evaluating all that we do, it's names like these that are an important part of the ultimate measure of whether we are doing good or great.

JOINING THE JOURNEY

MAYBE IT'S BECAUSE ANNA AND I FIRST MET while walking, but I have this dream about one day following, on foot, one of Europe's historic pilgrimage routes, from the Pyrenees mountains to Santiago de Compostela in Spain, taking a month to disconnect from our busy lives, slow down, and renew. Anna likes the theory but needs more persuading.

I daydream about it sometimes when I am on one of my fitness walks and I have done some reading about the trail we have in mind. The trail is well worn, and I've collected lots of advice from people who have gone before.

The performance philanthropy path I have been on with Geneva Global has been less well marked. There have been pointers in places, but for the most part, it has felt like carving a new trail.

Unlike the pilgrim route of El Camino I have in mind, there was no clear destination when I set out, but, as they say, the longest journey starts with the first step. And following that beginning, there have been some missteps along the way.

The path to performance philanthropy has been, in turn, demanding, exhausting, exhilarating, and above all, incredibly rewarding. There have been shocks, surprises, and significant impact.

It can be hard work blending head and heart. I have met people in desperate circumstances all over the world, but I never fail to be touched by their situation. I still shed tears. But at the same time, I know that to truly serve them well we need to pursue the best programs. It requires being compassionate and dispassionate, keeping faith with the vision, and being willing to face the brutal facts.

Having good fellow travelers on the journey has been crucial. Finding the way ahead in performance philanthropy owes so much to the foresight of Christopher and Richard Chandler, whose desire to make a bigger difference led to the founding of Geneva Global.

Though they passed that baton on to me, Christopher continues to be closely involved with Geneva Global. His Legatum Foundation looks to us to advise its activities, which have given more than eighty million dollars to over 1,400 projects in over one hundred countries since 1999.

Geneva Global and the Legatum Foundation have journeyed together, learning how to pursue performance philanthropy. And we have been joined by many others along the way.

I hope that, having read this book, you may have been encouraged to think about how you can begin a similar journey in doing good great. I or a member of my team would be delighted to have the opportunity to speak with you about how we might join with you in your journey and begin to partner in changing the world.

YOU CAN CONTACT US AT:

Geneva Global
Telephone: +1 (610) 254 0000
www.genevaglobal.com

ACKNOWLEDGMENTS

A book like this one—of stories, memories, and lessons—always has a cast of characters in it that never gets all the credit they are due. I owe so much to so many.

First off, I'd like to thank Andy Butcher, who skillfully brought my stories and ideas to light and so expertly crafted them for this book.

To Ava Lala, Geneva Global's marketing director who has seen this project through to completion; Jenn Richey Nicholas, who worked on the book design; Anne Dubuisson, who helped advise and edit; and numerous Geneva Global stars, all of whom had to learn more about my life than they ever wanted to know: a big thank you!

Then my thanks go to the Geneva Global team, whose work is described throughout this book. They are the ones who take a concept and bring it into being on the ground—truly a creative labor of love. I want to give a particular shout-out to the original team who took the risk of gambling their futures on whether we could create a new way of transforming lives in a philanthropic space that is not known for its business success. In particular, Karen Robinson, our CFO, who took a call from Dubai and committed to our start-up environment after only having known me for a few months.

To all our implementing partners around the world, your selflessness, dedication, and heroism are truly humbling. You are making a difference in the lives of your neighbors and communities, and we are inspired each and every day by what you do.

I want to warmly thank Christopher Chandler, Alan McCormick, Mark Stoleson, Philip Vassiliou, and everyone at Legatum, who have been wonderful colearners and companions on this exciting journey to date. I owe so much to Christopher, in particular, for letting me take a shot at building a social enterprise out of his philanthropy vehicle. I look forward to all we can continue to innovate together on in the future.

To Ellen Agler and friends at the END Fund, Nick Grono and friends at the Freedom Fund, and other members of the wider Legatum family, I just want to affirm the amazing work you are doing and the creative ways you are aggregating capital for such world-changing work. It is an honor to work alongside you.

Geneva Global's clients are amazing philanthropists and thinkers, and we would not have the privilege of doing what we do if it weren't for them and the trust they place in us. I am grateful for your passion and generosity in wanting to make a difference in the lives of people around the world.

This story started a long time before my arrival at Geneva Global in late 2005. So much of what I learned at De Beers, Cranfield School of Management, Buckmaster & Moore, Lucas Engineering & Systems, Youth With A Mission, Medair, Tearfund, Micah Network, and Integral came from my mistakes, and in this, I had some very patient and supportive bosses, guides, mentors, and formative examples. In particular, I would like to highlight and honor Alec Medlycott, Mike Wyatt, Ian White, John Parnaby, Floyd McClung, Warren Lancaster, Graham Fairbairn, Jennie Collins, Brian Chilver, Tony Faulkner, Steve Bradbury, Fiona Boshoff, and many friends in both the Micah and Integral families.

And then thanks go to my family—my mum and my sister, Janet—who have been forever supportive in all the crazy places and ideas I've had and taught me that all I could and should do was my best. To my kids, Lexi, Jon, and Ryan: three better human beings I could not have imagined having as offspring. I can't tell you enough how proud I am of each one of you. And Anna, you don't get more praise, as the dedication was enough, and it will go to your head!

Finally, at seventeen, I took a decision to hand over my life to the Trinity of God the Father, Jesus, my role model, and the Holy Spirit. Bearing in mind my life trajectory at the time and my ability to mess things up when I have chosen to try and run things on my own, I consider the fact that almost anything worthwhile in this book and my life as a whole is down to God's great unconditional love, patience, and being able to see in me what I could not see in myself. To you I owe everything.

ABOUT THE AUTHORS

DOUG BALFOUR is owner and CEO of Geneva Global. He provides expert guidance to foundations, corporations, individuals, and other organizations throughout the world that seek to apply a business mind-set and results-oriented approach to their social-impact efforts.

With more than twenty-five years of experience in philanthropy, international development, leadership, and organizational development, Doug brings a wealth of knowledge to his work with Geneva Global's clients. Since taking ownership of Geneva Global in 2008, Doug has assembled a leadership team that brings expertise from the worlds of international development, global health, finance, consulting, risk management, and marketing to each client assignment.

Throughout his career, Doug has spoken on topics such as maximizing social impact, measuring social change, creating social transformation through collaboration, and the meeting of strategic philanthropy and impact investing. Currently, Doug sits on the boards of Capital for Good, USA; Capital for Good, UK; and the END Fund.

ANDY BUTCHER is an international journalist and writer who has traveled to forty countries, writing extensively about relief and development for newspapers, magazines, and organizations. His books include *Street Children: The Tragedy and Challenge of the World's Millions of Modern-Day Oliver Twists*. www.andybutcheronline.com.

Made in the USA
Middletown, DE
14 January 2015